Racial Profiling

Other Books in the Current Controversies Series

Racial Profiling

Noël Merino, Book Editor

GREENHAVEN PRESS
A part of Gale, Cengage Learning

GALE
CENGAGE Learning·

Farmington Hills, Mich • San Francisco • New York • Waterville, Maine
Meriden, Conn • Mason, Ohio • Chicago

Elizabeth Des Chenes, *Director, Content Strategy*
Douglas Dentino, *Manager, New Product*

© 2015 Greenhaven Press, a part of Gale, Cengage Learning

WCN: 01-100-101

Gale and Greenhaven Press are registered trademarks used herein under license.

For more information, contact:
Greenhaven Press
27500 Drake Rd.
Farmington Hills, MI 48331-3535
Or you can visit our Internet site at gale.cengage.com

Articles in Greenhaven Press anthologies are often edited for length to meet page requirements. In addition, original titles of these works are changed to clearly present the main thesis and to explicitly indicate the author's opinion. Every effort is made to ensure that Greenhaven Press accurately reflects the original intent of the authors. Every effort has been made to trace the owners of copyrighted material.

Cover image © Tony Savino/Corbis.

LIBRARY OF CONGRESS CATALOGING-IN-PUBLICATION DATA

Racial profiling / Noël Merino, book editor.
    pages cm. -- (Current controversies)
    Includes bibliographical references and index.
    ISBN 978-0-7377-7223-4 (hardcover) -- ISBN 978-0-7377-7224-1 (pbk.)
    1. Racial profiling in law enforcement. 2. Discrimination in law enforcement. I. Merino, Noël, editor of compilation.
    HV7936.R3R36 2015
    363.2'3089--dc23
                                            2014021949

Printed in the United States of America
1 2 3 4 5 6 7 18 17 16 15 14

Contents

The US Justice Department's investigations of racial profiling in city police departments ignore racial crime rates and harm minority communities. Such federal oversight drains the limited resources of local police departments and hampers their ability to fight crime.

Chapter 2: Should Arab Muslims Be Profiled in the War on Terror?

Yes: Arab Muslims Should Be Profiled in the War on Terror

The trial and acquittal of George Zimmerman illustrates the pervasive racism against African Americans in the criminal justice system and the media, which is reminiscent of slavery or the treatment of blacks during the Jim Crow era.

Chapter 4: What Should Be Done About Racial Profiling?

Legal restrictions on racial profiling need to be carefully constructed and limited to race and ethnicity, but with exceptions for national security operations. Thus, new guidelines being considered by the US Department of Justice that expand the definition of racial profiling and increase the categories protected beyond race and ethnicity should be opposed.

Foreword

By definition, controversies are "discussions of questions in which opposing opinions clash" (*Webster's Twentieth Century Dictionary Unabridged*). Few would deny that controversies are a pervasive part of the human condition and exist on virtually every level of human enterprise. Controversies transpire between individuals and among groups, within nations and between nations. Controversies supply the grist necessary for progress by providing challenges and challengers to the status quo. They also create atmospheres where strife and warfare can flourish. A world without controversies would be a peaceful world; but it also would be, by and large, static and prosaic.

The Series' Purpose

The purpose of the Current Controversies series is to explore many of the social, political, and economic controversies dominating the national and international scenes today. Titles selected for inclusion in the series are highly focused and specific. For example, from the larger category of criminal justice, Current Controversies deals with specific topics such as police brutality, gun control, white collar crime, and others. The debates in Current Controversies also are presented in a useful, timeless fashion. Articles and book excerpts included in each title are selected if they contribute valuable, long-range ideas to the overall debate. And wherever possible, current information is enhanced with historical documents and other relevant materials. Thus, while individual titles are current in focus, every effort is made to ensure that they will not become quickly outdated. Books in the Current Controversies series will remain important resources for librarians, teachers, and students for many years.

In addition to keeping the titles focused and specific, great care is taken in the editorial format of each book in the series. Book introductions and chapter prefaces are offered to provide background material for readers. Chapters are organized around several key questions that are answered with diverse opinions representing all points on the political spectrum. Materials in each chapter include opinions in which authors clearly disagree as well as alternative opinions in which authors may agree on a broader issue but disagree on the possible solutions. In this way, the content of each volume in Current Controversies mirrors the mosaic of opinions encountered in society. Readers will quickly realize that there are many viable answers to these complex issues. By questioning each author's conclusions, students and casual readers can begin to develop the critical thinking skills so important to evaluating opinionated material.

Current Controversies is also ideal for controlled research. Each anthology in the series is composed of primary sources taken from a wide gamut of informational categories including periodicals, newspapers, books, US and foreign government documents, and the publications of private and public organizations. Readers will find factual support for reports, debates, and research papers covering all areas of important issues. In addition, an annotated table of contents, an index, a book and periodical bibliography, and a list of organizations to contact are included in each book to expedite further research.

Perhaps more than ever before in history, people are confronted with diverse and contradictory information. During the Persian Gulf War, for example, the public was not only treated to minute-to-minute coverage of the war, it was also inundated with critiques of the coverage and countless analyses of the factors motivating US involvement. Being able to sort through the plethora of opinions accompanying today's major issues, and to draw one's own conclusions, can be a complicated and frustrating struggle. It is the editors' hope that Current Controversies will help readers with this struggle.

Introduction

"Racial profiling involves targeting an entire group of people for suspicion based on the group's race, ethnicity, religion, or national origin."

In the debate about racial profiling, one of the key starting points for discussion is the definition of racial profiling. The National Institute of Justice defines it this way:

> Racial profiling by law enforcement is commonly defined as a practice that targets people for suspicion of crime based on their race, ethnicity, religion or national origin. Creating a profile about the kinds of people who commit certain types of crimes may lead officers to generalize about a particular group and act according to the generalization rather than specific behavior.

The American Civil Liberties Union (ACLU) notes the difference between racial profiling and criminal profiling:

> "Racial Profiling" refers to the discriminatory practice by law enforcement officials of targeting individuals for suspicion of crime based on the individual's race, ethnicity, religion or national origin. Criminal profiling, generally, as practiced by police, is the reliance on a group of characteristics they believe to be associated with crime.

The ACLU notes that criminal profiling is a legitimate practice of law enforcement: "Racial profiling does not refer to the act of a law enforcement agent pursuing a suspect in which the specific description of the suspect includes race or ethnicity in combination with other identifying factors." Thus, racial profiling involves targeting an entire group of people for suspicion based on the group's race, ethnicity, religion, or national origin.

One concern about racial profiling in law enforcement is that it is ineffective. For example, imagine the police department of a particular American city assumed drug dealers would be black males in their teens and twenties. This might lead to law enforcement behavior that would single out young, black males for traffic stops, frisks, and surveillance in a manner that was both under- and over-inclusive: drug dealers could be older white males or young Hispanic females—among others—so the policy would be "under-inclusive," passing over legitimate suspects because of the assumption of racial profiling. Additionally, most young black males are not drug dealers, so the law enforcement strategy would be "over-inclusive," targeting innocent people with suspicion. Furthermore, as the National Institute of Justice notes, "racial profiling is unlikely to be an effective policing strategy as criminals can simply shift their activities outside the profile." If only young, black males are under suspicion for dealing drugs, then it makes sense to move the drug trade into the hands of young, white females and other demographic groups to avoid detection.

Another concern about racial profiling in law enforcement is that it violates civil rights. The ACLU says, "Racial profiling continues to be a prevalent and egregious form of discrimination in the United States. This unjustifiable practice remains a stain on American democracy and an affront to the promise of racial equality." There is a concern that racial profiling unfairly targets minority groups, operating as a bias in law enforcement activities. The Fourteenth Amendment to the US Constitution guarantees that no state shall "deprive any person of life, liberty, or property, without due process of law; nor deny to any person within its jurisdiction the equal protection of the laws." Critics of racial profiling are concerned that the targets of racial profiling are not given equal protection of the laws.

Even though there are widespread concerns about racial profiling, not everyone agrees that it is a common practice in the United States. Some argue that law enforcement is unfairly accused of racial profiling when, in fact, they are engaging in legitimate criminal profiling. Additionally, when crime statistics are disproportionally higher for a particular racial or ethnic group, some maintain that targeting this group for enhanced crime surveillance does not constitute egregious racial profiling. Thus, for instance, if young, black males are disproportionately involved in drug dealing, there are those who argue that profiling young, black males in drug law enforcement is one legitimate part of police work on this issue.

Thus, even with a consensus on the definition of racial profiling, there is no consensus on whether or not racial profiling constitutes a large problem in the United States or whether action needs to be taken to halt law enforcement practices that profile according to race, ethnicity, religion, and national origin. These debates and others are explored in *Current Controversies: Racial Profiling*.

CHAPTER 1

Is Racial Profiling a Problem?

Chapter Preface

Racial profiling may or may not be a problem in the United States: the answer depends on how much racial profiling actually exists and one's perception of the permissible uses of racial profiling in carrying out law enforcement activities. In the United States, surveys of various racial groups show a marked difference in perceptions about police fairness toward racial groups. In addition, a majority of Americans seem to find racial profiling unproblematic when related to national security, such as with air travel or protecting cities and national landmarks.

Gallup's *Minority Rights and Relations* poll, conducted in July 2013, found that 24 percent of black men under the age of 35 said that the police had treated them unfairly during the past thirty days. Among black males aged 35 to 54, 22 percent said they had been treated unfairly in recent weeks. A *Washington Post*-ABC News poll conducted that same month found that 86 percent of African Americans think that blacks and other minorities do not receive equal treatment as whites in the criminal justice system. In contrast, only 41 percent of whites thought that blacks and other minorities do not receive equal treatment.

When asked specifically about their thoughts about racial profiling in airports to stop terrorists, the vast majority of Americans appear to find the practice unproblematic. A *USA Today*/Gallup poll in January 2010 found that 71 percent of Americans favor the practice of subjecting airline passengers who fit the profile of terrorists—based on their age, ethnicity, or gender—to special, more intensive security checks before boarding US flights. Only 21 percent opposed the practice, with the remainder unsure.

Racial profiling in the United States is a contentious issue with respect to counterterrorism activities, law enforcement practices, and immigration enforcement. As the viewpoints of this chapter illustrate, there is a wide diversity of opinions on the issue of racial profiling in the United States and conflicting views about whether racial profiling is a problem.

How the Hunt for Bin Laden Made US Muslims and Immigrants Threats

Seth Freed Wessler

Seth Freed Wessler is an investigative reporter for Colorlines.

Ten years after Sept. 11, 2001, the animating target of the war on terror is dead, his body cast into the sea. A chapter is closed. Yet, in many communities here in the United States, it seemed the target was never just Osama bin Laden. For Arabs and Muslims in the U.S., and for those lumped carelessly together with them, the war on terrorism has not been an abstraction waged in far off lands, but a fight that's engulfed communities right here at home.

In the long decade since Al Qaeda accomplished the unthinkable, slaughtering thousands and ushering in a global war that's taken countless more lives, the U.S. has massively expanded anti-terrorism operations within our own borders. The homeland security infrastructure quickly erected in the attack's aftermath regularly targets men and women who have nothing to do with terrorism, while making racial profiling and mass deportation a regular feature of life.

Less than a month after 9/11, George W. Bush launched the Office of Homeland Security, which would soon become the Department of Homeland Security. As the Department of Defense led our military into one, two, and then three wars, the Department of Homeland Security was charged with defending against the barbarians at the gates, or worse, those already in our midst. To fight the menace, DHS consolidated more than 20 agencies into one mamouth department.

Perhaps the most consequential element of this bureaucratic shift was the decision to move the regulation of immigration and borders into the realm of anti-terrorism. Overnight, decisions about who would be allowed to enter and who would be forced to leave were refracted through a lens of national security. Non-citizens and those traveling through our ports became threats by definition—people to be secured against.

Racial Profiling as National Security

Muslims in the U.S. became the most ominous threat, by policy. The Department of Homeland Security created the National Security Entry-Exit Registration System (NSEERS), commonly called "Special Registration," which functioned as a deportation net specifically for Muslims. As *Colorlines'* Channing Kennedy wrote in April:

> Initiated in September 2002, NSEERS functioned like Arizona's SB 1070, with working-class Muslims as the target. Its first phase required all non-citizen male residents, ages 16 to 65, from a list of "suspect" nations, to register at INS offices. Thousands of families went out of their way to comply with the law, thinking it would be part of the government-sponsored pathways to citizenship that they were already participating in. Instead, in July 2003, the *Washington Post* reported it as the deportation of "the largest number of visitors from Middle Eastern and other Muslim countries in U.S. history—more than 13,000 of the nearly 83,000 men older than 16 who complied with the registration program by various deadlines between last September and April."

Last week, the federal government officially ended the NSEERS program. That, says Dawud Walid, executive director of the Council on American-Islamic Relations in Michigan, "is hugely important. A victory. But we have a long, long way."

Indeed, a new report released today jointly by the Center for Human Rights and Global Justice at the NYU Law School and the Asian American Legal Defense Fund (AALDEF) finds that even without the explicit racial and religious targeting built into Special Registration, the Department of Homeland Security continues to push Muslims into detention and deportation in equally insidious, but less formal ways.

After 9/11 the Bush administration was more than clear that it would use the immigration legal system to target people they deemed to be possible threats.

Tareq Abu Fayad, a young Saudi man profiled in the report, has been detained for four years, since trying to enter the country with a *valid* immigration visa. Agents at the San Francisco airport deemed him a possible terrorist threat because he had saved Al Jazeera articles and September 11 conspiracy theory series on his laptop. He was ordered deported. He appealed the ruling, but a circuit court upheld the order.

Sameer Ahmed, an attorney at AALDEF, explains, "After 9/11 the Bush administration was more than clear that it would use the immigration legal system to target people they deemed to be possible threats. The reason they decided to do this, rather than to only use the criminal system, is that the immigration system does not afford individuals the same rights and due process that exist in criminal law."

Fayad could never have been tried criminally because he'd never done anything to warrant criminal charges, but in immigration court the government can have him removed.

"We're seeing a trend where Muslims are being deported, detained and denied entry into the United States for no good reason except tenuous affiliations or unsubstantiated claims," said Ahmed.

Borders and airports are often the points where noncitizens are first detained. Muslims and Arabs now face a dense layer of racial profiling when traveling through airports and borders. Dawud Walid of CAIR explains that for communities in and around Detroit and Dearborn, Mich., which has one of the county's largest Arab populations, "the issues at the border with border patrol are huge. People coming back from Canada and some are detained for hours, cuffed and asked questions about religious practice, about how many times they pray, ridiculous questions that have nothing to do with crime."

That's because they have committed no crime.

The FBI's Manufactured Threats

Of course, in the absence of actual crimes and real threats, the massive domestic security apparatus has simply created them. The FBI, in its search for "homegrown" Bin Ladens, has repeatedly used secret informant-instigators to manufacture terrorist plots and then entice disaffected young men of color to get involved.

According to a 2010 investigation by *Democracy Now!*, an FBI informant allegedly entrapped four black Muslim men from a poor neighborhood in Newburgh, N.Y., pushing them to participate in a concocted attack on a synagogue in the area.

Now that U.S. forces have killed [Osama bin Laden], Muslim communities in the U.S. are left wondering what happens next.

The government argues that the Newburgh men's participation in the fake plot proves that they were predisposed to terrorism. "Those who characterize the FBI's activities in this case as 'entrapment' simply do not have their facts straight—or do not have a full understanding of the law," Attorney General Eric Holder said. But the defense contends that the men would never have committed any act of violence were it not for the FBI's fabrication of a plot and its concerted campaign to convince them to join it.

The broad use of manufactured plots and informants are not the Department of Justice's only shady homeland security practices. A recent investigation in the *Washington Monthly* digs into the world of unchecked anti-terrorism training programs for local and state government. The programs, funded with billions in federal dollars, are often run by sideshow figures that make their money purportedly teaching local cops how to spot a terrorist. In one such class in Florida, 60 cops listened as a private-sector anti-terrorism "expert" explained Islam and how to deal with Muslims:

> "Anyone who says that Islam is a religion of peace is either ignorant or flat out lying. . . . The best way to handle these people is what I call legal harassment."

The training efforts, which is one of many around the country, fit squarely within a set of Department of Justice programs meant to use local police to report "suspicious activity" to the feds—suspicious activity explained by an unabashed islamophobe.

All of this is the legacy of our government's hunt for Bin Laden. Now that U.S. forces have killed him, Muslim communities in the U.S. are left wondering what happens next.

"This is a time for closure for the victims of 9/11 and in fact for all victims of terrorism all over the world," said Hassan Jaber, the director of an Arab American social services organization in Dearborn called ACCESS. "The conversation after 9/11, that there is a clash of civilizations, really that was never the case and that theory did not work in real life."

There are sadly few signs, however, that the internal security apparatus constructed to meet that post-9/11 view of the world will die with Bin Laden.

"I think the targeting of Muslims has gotten worse during the Obama administration," says Dawud Walid of CAIR. "Just recently, FBI interrogations, which many people call fishing expeditions, have occurred and we have had people [in Michigan] who were asked by the FBI about their political viewpoints about what's happening in Arab countries, in the so-called Arab Spring."

The search for terrorists continues.

Racial Profiling Is Being Used in Immigration Checks

Aura Bogado

Aura Bogado writes about racial justice, Native rights, and immigration for The Nation.

David de la Fuente might still be alive if his pal David Salazar hadn't been short on cash one day. Both men lived in Phoenix [Arizona], where they'd settled after making their separate ways north from the Mexican farming village of Colonia Emilio Carranza many years earlier. Salazar and his family came across legally in 1974, while de la Fuente arrived during the 1990s, traversing the desert on foot to cross the border illegally near Nogales, Arizona. De la Fuente, a plumber, and Salazar, a delivery driver, eventually became good friends. Their families grew close, too, often spending weekends and holidays together.

But that all changed one morning in May 2009, when Salazar asked de la Fuente for a ride to the ATM. They hopped into de la Fuente's green Nissan Maxima and drove to a nearby Wells Fargo. As they were about to turn into the parking lot, a Phoenix squad car driving behind them hit its flashers.

An Arrest in Arizona

By Salazar's account, officer Matthew Prutch asked de la Fuente for a driver's license. When he produced a fake, Prutch had him step out of the car and handcuffed him. Salazar asked the officer whether he'd pulled them over because of their skin color; Prutch, he says, replied that he was just doing his job. (In his report, Prutch wrote that he ran the Nissan's plates while following the car and found no driver's license data associated with the registered owner. "He appeared to be a Hispanic male," Prutch added, "and under reasonable suspicion I believe [sic] the driver to be driving with no valid license.") Minutes later, another officer arrived and asked Salazar for his license, even though he hadn't been at the wheel. Prutch then delivered de la Fuente to the police station for booking. From there, the 35-year-old was taken to Maricopa County Sherriff Joe Arpaio's notorious Durango Jail, and charged with using a fake ID. A month later, he was dead.

Before SB 1070, the Arizona law that allows police officers to detain anyone they suspect might be in the country without papers, there was 287(g). That's a 1996 amendment to the Immigration and Nationality Act under which the feds can deputize state and local law enforcement to capture and detain undocumented immigrants. Some 71 agencies in 26 states operate under 287(g) agreements—Arpaio signed up in 2007.

The man who calls himself "America's toughest sheriff" has long had a knack for drawing media attention—reviving chain gangs, for instance, and humiliating county inmates by forcing them to don pink underwear. He grew obsessed with illegal immigration in 2005, when the state's "coyote statute" took effect, making it a felony to smuggle people for profit anywhere in Arizona. As interpreted by then-county prosecutor Andrew Thomas, the law freed sheriff's deputies to round up undocumented immigrants—after all, hadn't these people conspired to smuggle themselves into Arizona? So Arpaio began sending out posses of citizens and lawmen to conduct immigration sweeps. "I'm not going to turn these people over to federal authorities so they can have a free ride back to Mexico," he told the *Washington Times*. "I'll give them a free ride to my jail."

A Sheriff's Focus on Immigration

It was Arpaio's zeal that compelled me to spend five months on his home turf last year. I wanted to see firsthand how his tactics affected the Latino residents who make up 31 percent of the county's population. I heard story after story—from citizens, legal immigrants, and undocumented residents alike—about encounters with deputies and cops determined to play Border Patrol. It got to the point where I raced home in a panic one morning after heading out for a jog without ID—what if a deputy, seeing a Latina running down the street, decided to haul me in?

To most anyone who even looks Latino in Maricopa County, the long arm of the sheriff seems inescapable.

Native Americans told me they were targeted because deputies mistook them for Latinos. Latinos told me of being stopped randomly on the street and shouted at—or worse—by officers demanding identification. Alex, a third-generation US citizen, was at a Circle K buying water while his parents waited outside. He ran out when he heard a group of Arpaio's deputies yelling at them to produce their papers. Then, Alex said, they demanded to see his ID, too, explaining, "The law says everyone here has to be legal." (Fearing retaliation, Alex asked that we not use his real name.)

Then there was Celia Alejandra Álvarez, who told me deputies broke her jaw during a raid at the landscaping company she worked for. Álvarez said she was denied adequate medical care during her three-month detention—a common complaint that has been the subject of hundreds of lawsuits against Arpaio. Even after surgery, she added, her jaw still isn't back to normal—during our interview she paused periodically to readjust it. (In 2008, the National Commission on Correctional Health Care yanked Maricopa County's accreditation, saying its jails failed to meet national standards.)

Maurilio (who also feared giving his real name) is a construction worker who has lived in the United States without papers for 21 years, raising two kids who are US citizens. He said his family was camping at a lake over the Fourth of July weekend in 2008, when a fellow camper started yelling something about "too many Mexicans" and called the sheriff's office. The deputies, Maurilio and his wife told me, threw him down in the presence of his six-year-old son and shoved his face into the ground. They then yanked his head up by his hair and pepper-sprayed him as they cuffed him. After a few weeks at Durango, he was deported—and immediately headed to the desert to walk back north.

To most anyone who even looks Latino in Maricopa County, the long arm of the sheriff seems inescapable. Indeed, Arpaio's tactics have put his agency at the center of an ongoing civil rights investigation by the Department of Justice. In the fall of 2009, without explanation, the Department of Homeland Security rescinded Arpaio's authority to arrest people under section 287(g)—although deputies can still check the immigration status of people arriving at the jails. In anticipation of the crackdown, Arpaio held a press conference. "We have arrested 1,600 illegals that have not committed any crime other than being here illegally," he boasted. "The secret is, we're still going to do the same thing—we have the state laws, and by the way, we'll still enforce the federal laws without the oversight, the policy, the restrictions that they put on us."

The Death of de la Fuente

When David de la Fuente arrived at Durango, his friends and family say, deputies immediately began grilling him about his immigration status. One of his sisters visited twice, as did Salazar. Each told me that de la Fuente was deteriorating quickly. The guards, he told them, kept dragging him back and forth between the prison yard (where temperatures reached 107 degrees) and the frigid jail—leaving him queasy and disoriented. He also complained of severe chest pains, but fearing the guards might retaliate, told his family not to press the authorities about his condition. Eventually, de la Fuente was hauled before a judge, who fined him and put him on probation for giving an alias to the police. After three weeks in custody, he was turned over to federal immigration authorities, who delivered him the next day to Nogales, Mexico, about 700 miles north of his hometown. By that time, he was gravely ill.

He arrived in Colonia Emilio Carranza three days later, stumbling and barely able to speak. His family got him to the hospital, where he was diagnosed with acute pneumonia. Based on the stage of his illness, the doctors determined that de la Fuente had contracted it about 15 days earlier—roughly a week into his jail stay—according to medical paperwork and an interview with the hospital director. The doctors did what they could, but de la Fuente was too far gone. His cousins and a sister stood vigil as he dwindled and eventually fell into a coma. He was pronounced dead on June 23—exactly four weeks after the traffic stop.

We may never know what exactly happened to David de la Fuente inside Durango. To see his health records, family members would have to file a signed release and affidavit—something they are, not surprisingly, scared to do. What is clear is that Arpaio's flavor of law enforcement will spread around the state if the ACLU [American Civil Liberties Union] (which filed suit in May 2010) fails to stop SB 1070 from taking effect. [In 2012, the US Supreme Court upheld the provision of SB 1070 allowing state police to investigate immigration status.] "The intent of the law was that it would be used disproportionately against people who have certain physical attributes," notes Michael Wishnie, a professor at Yale Law School. "Police on the ground understand that and will act accordingly."

This past September [2009], during my visit to Colonia Emilio Carranza, Norberto Alvarado Santana said little as he showed me his cousin's grave, in a humble cemetery adorned with plastic flowers and Virgen de Guadalupe figurines. A stout, reserved man, he measured his words cautiously before finally breaking the silence. "There's a word for what happened to my cousin David," he said. "It's homicide."

Racial Profiling Is a Rational Response to Information

Walter E. Williams

Walter E. Williams is the John M. Olin Distinguished Professor of Economics at George Mason University in Fairfax, Virginia, and a syndicated columnist.

Harvard Professor Henry Gates' arrest [in July 2009, in Cambridge, Massachusetts] has given new life to the issue of racial profiling. We can think of profiling in general as a practice where people use an observable or known physical attribute as a proxy or estimator of some other unobservable or unknown attribute. Race or sex profiling is simply the use of race or sex as that estimator. Profiling represents mankind's attempt to cope with information cost. God would not have to profile since God is all knowing.

Racial Profiling in Medicine

People differ by race and sex. Let's look at a few profiling examples to see which ones you'd like outlawed. According to the American Cancer Society, the lifetime risk of men getting breast cancer is about 1/10th of 1 percent, or 1 in 1,000; and 440 men will die of breast cancer this year. For women, the risk of developing breast cancer is about 12 percent, or 1 in 8, and 40,610 will die from it this year. Should doctors and medical insurance companies be prosecuted for the discriminatory practice of routine breast cancer screening for women but not for men?

Some racial and ethnic groups have higher incidence and mortality from various diseases than the national average. The rates of death from cardiovascular diseases are about 30 percent higher among black adults than among white adults. Cervical cancer rates are five times higher among Vietnamese women in the U.S. than among white women. Pima Indians of Arizona have the highest known diabetes rates in the world. Prostate cancer is nearly twice as common among black men as white men.

Knowing patient race or ethnicity, what might be considered as racial profiling, can assist medical providers in the delivery of more effective medical services.

Racial Profiling in Assessing Criminality

One might take the position that while it is acceptable for doctors to use race, ethnicity and sex as indicators of the higher probability of certain diseases, it is not acceptable to use race or ethnicity as indicators for other attributes such as criminal behavior. Other than simply stating that it is acceptable to use race or ethnicity as an information acquisition technique in the case of medicine but not in other areas of life, is there really a difference? Surely, race and ethnicity are not perfect indicators of the risk of prostate cancer or hypertension; neither are they perfect indicators of criminal behavior; however, there are concrete factual data that surely indicate associations. Criminologist Marvin Wolfgang says, "For four violent offenses—homicide, rape, robbery and aggravated assault—the crime rates for blacks are at least 10 times as high as they are for whites."

In a 1999 article, "Capital Cabbies Salute Race Profiling," James Owens writes, "If racial profiling is racism, then the cab drivers of Washington, D.C., they themselves mainly blacks and Hispanics, are all for it. A District taxicab commissioner, Sandra Seegars, who is black, issued a safety-advice statement urging D.C.'s 6,800 cabbies to refuse to pick up 'dangerous looking' passengers. She described 'dangerous looking' as a young black guy ... with shirttail hanging down longer than his coat, baggy pants, unlaced tennis shoes."

The *Pizza Marketing Quarterly* carried a story of charges of racial discrimination filed in St. Louis [Missouri] against Papa John's pizza delivery services. Papa John's district manager said she could not and would not ask her drivers to put their lives on the line. She added that the racial discrimination accusation is false because 75 to 85 percent of the drivers in the complaining neighborhood are black and, moreover, most of those drivers lived in the very neighborhood being denied delivery service.

Some years ago, the Rev. Jesse Jackson complained, "There is nothing more painful to me at this stage in my life than to walk down the street and hear footsteps and start thinking about robbery—then look around and see somebody white and feel relieved."

Here's my question: Is the racial profiling done by cab drivers, pizza deliverers or Jesse Jackson a sign of racism or economizing on information costs?

Racial Disparities in Police Activity Do Not Indicate Racial Profiling

Heather Mac Donald

Heather Mac Donald is a John M. Olin Fellow at the Manhattan Institute, a contributing editor to City Journal, *and author of* Are Cops Racist? How the War Against the Police Harms Black Americans.

In 2000, a deputy attorney general in the [Bill] Clinton administration slapped the Los Angeles Police Department [LAPD] with federal oversight. A 1994 law gives the Justice Department the authority to seek control of police agencies that have engaged in a "pattern or practice" of constitutional violations. Justice's attorneys never uncovered any systemic constitutional abuses in the LAPD as required by the 1994 law, despite having commandeered hundreds of thousands of documents (and having lost 10 boxes of sensitive records). Nevertheless, for the next decade the LAPD would operate under a draconian federal "consent decree"—a nominally consensual agreement overseen by a court—governing nearly every aspect of its operations, at a cost of over $100 million in contracting fees and in manpower diverted to mindless paper-pushing.

The Justice Department's Police Oversight

The deputy attorney general who forced federal control on the LAPD in 2000 was none other than Eric Holder, who now presides over a Justice Department determined to make the Los Angeles consent decree the model for its future oversight of police departments. The current assistant attorney general for civil rights, Thomas Perez, told a conference of police chiefs in June 2010 that the Justice Department would be pursuing "pattern or practice" takeovers of police departments much more aggressively than the [George W.] Bush administration, eschewing negotiation in favor of hardball tactics seeking immediate federal control. Perez has hired nine additional attorneys to beef up his division's search for alleged police agency racism and to sue agencies that don't capitulate to federal demands.

To see what lies ahead for the nation's police, one need look no further than the Los Angeles Police Department's past and present travails with the Justice Department [DOJ].

The LAPD consent decree was a power grab from day one. The first thing DOJ demanded as part of its new authority over the LAPD was the collection of racial information on every stop the L.A. officers make—even though the corruption scandal which provided the pretext for the consent decree had nothing to do with race or alleged "racial profiling."

The LAPD is arguably the most professional, community-oriented police agency in the country.

The 180-clause decree mired the LAPD's operations in red tape, apparently on the theory that if cops are left to actually fight crime, rather than writing and reviewing reports, they will run amok violating people's rights. Today, an L.A. officer can hardly nod at a civilian without filling out numerous forms documenting his salutation for later review. If he returns fire at a gangbanger, his use of force will be more intensely investigated for wrong-doing than the criminal shooting that provoked the officer's defensive reaction in the first place.

The LAPD spent approximately $40 million trying to comply with the decree in its first year and close to $50 million annually for several years thereafter. It pulled 350 officers off the street to meet the decree's mountainous paperwork requirements. Nevertheless, it struggled to meet the fanatical standards for compliance imposed by the federal monitor overseeing the decree, who demanded that virtually 100 percent of the arbitrary deadlines for filing reports be met on time, regardless of whether the supervisors who missed their deadline by a few days were otherwise occupied with a triple homicide investigation. In 2006, the federal court to which the monitor reported deemed the department out of compliance with the decree and extended its term. In 2009, the court ended federal control on many of the decree's provisions, yet continued federal oversight on issues relating to "biased policing," among other matters, until January 2011. And now the Justice Department, facing the potential final expiration of the consent decree this month, has made its most preposterous charge against the LAPD yet, in a desperate last-minute bid to retain its power over the force.

According to DOJ's civil rights division, the LAPD does not investigate racial profiling complaints with sufficient intensity. The department seems to tolerate a "culture that is inimical to race-neutral policing," say the federal attorneys. These accusations are nothing short of delusional. The LAPD is arguably the most professional, community-oriented police agency in the country, having been led for most of the last decade by modern policing's premier innovator, William Bratton. Moreover, it investigates every racial profiling allegation with an obsessive thoroughness that stands in stark contrast to the frivolity of most profiling accusations. There is no racial profiling complaint so patently fabricated that the department won't subject to days of painstaking investigation through multiple chains of command. A complainant can outright admit making up the profiling charge in retaliation for being arrested, and the LAPD's special profiling investigation body, the Constitutional Policing Unit, will continue diligently poring over his complaint as if it had been made in good faith. After the department logs a whopping average of 100 hours on each complaint, devoting more resources to these knee-jerk accusations than to any other kind of alleged officer misbehavior, the LAPD's civilian inspector general will audit the department's work with a two-part, 60-question matrix, subjecting claims made by arresting officers to a reflexive skepticism unmoored from reality. The goal of this Byzantine process? To find any possible way not to dismiss complaints as unsubstantiated.

A Racial Profiling Allegation

A recent profiling allegation and its disposition are typical. A driver who had been cited for tinted windows denied in his racial profiling complaint that his windows were tinted and claimed that he was only stopped because he was black. He said that he was detained for an excessive 45 minutes. The arresting officers estimated that the stop lasted 15 minutes; electronic records revealed that it lasted a reasonable 18 minutes. Department personnel interviewed the complainant twice; the arresting officers were closely interrogated; and the Constitutional Policing Unit [CPU] canvassed local businesses around the stop for video of the interaction. The CPU then made an appointment to photograph the driver's car to confirm that his windows were not tinted; the driver failed to appear at the appointment and later called the LAPD to say that he wanted no further contact from the department on his profiling complaint.

Leaving aside the devastating hole that the complainant blew in his own credibility by withholding his car, the complaint was logically problematic to begin with. If the driver's windows *were* tinted, the cops could not have seen his race, especially since the stop occurred at midnight. Indeed, the complainant himself reported that he had to keep his window rolled down during the stop so that the officer could see into the vehicle. But if the windows were *not* tinted, it strains credulity that an officer would cite a driver for a violation that could be so easily disproven simply by presenting the car.

The career attorneys who investigate police departments for constitutional violations are possibly the most left-wing members of the standing federal bureaucracy.

Nevertheless, the LAPD's inspector general Nicole Bershon, after reviewing the voluminous case history, concluded that the accused officer should not be cleared of the profiling charge and that the department should reopen the investigation—though there was nothing more to investigate. Because the car's windows had not been inspected, she said, the officer's claim that he could not see the driver's race before stopping him could not be adjudicated. Bershon, however, rehabilitated the *driver's* credibility on a wholly speculative theory: Because the sergeant who logged the profiling charge asked the driver in passing if he was making the complaint to avoid paying the tinting fine, the complainant lost confidence in the process, Bershon hypothesizes, and as a result went AWOL [absent without leave] with his car. Of course, the complainant had already shown enough confidence in the process to sit for two interviews. It was only when it came time to present his car that his painful disillusionment, in Bershon's imaginary scenario, manifested itself.

Predictably, Bershon criticizes the intake sergeant for questioning the complainant's motives, however flippantly. In an ideal world, to be sure, no police officer would ever express the slightest personal opinion in his interactions with civilians. But a station house is not an ideal world; it is peopled with human beings whose daily exposure to the full, sorry range of human behavior breeds in them a certain degree of cynicism. Regrettably, that cynicism occasionally breaks through the surface. The notion of cutting officers any slack for such failings, which, in light of their public service, are in any case relatively minor, is of course out of the question.

It is this insanely credulous and costly process for investigating racial profiling complaints that the [Barack] Obama Justice Department claims to find insufficiently rigorous, in a disturbing harbinger for other police departments. The most damning flaw of the LAPD's elaborate anti-profiling apparatus, from DOJ's perspective, is that it corroborates almost none of the already minuscule number of racial profiling complaints that the department receives each year. (In 2009, the department received 219 racial profiling complaints out of nearly 200,000 arrests and over 580,000 citations.) To the Washington attorneys, the paucity of confirmed complaints proves that the investigative process is inadequate, if not in bad faith, since it is a given to the Justice Department staff that the LAPD, like every other police department, routinely violates people's rights. The possibility that the vast majority of Los Angeles officers are operating within the law is simply not acceptable.

The Reality of Racial Crime Rates

Such a preordained conclusion is not surprising, since the career attorneys who investigate police departments for constitutional violations are possibly the most left-wing members of the standing federal bureaucracy. They know, without any felt need for prolonged exposure to police work, that contemporary policing is shot through with bias. In 2002, for example, a career attorney in the policing litigation section tried to bury a rigorously designed study that showed that black drivers on the New Jersey Turnpike speed at twice the rate of white drivers, a finding of great relevance to DOJ's then-pending charge that the higher stop rate of black drivers on the turnpike was the exclusive result of biased policing by New Jersey State Troopers.

The speeding study was eventually leaked to the press, and the attorney who had tried so hard to suppress it—to the point of hiding its conclusions from his political bosses—resigned. The career staffers who remained, however, were just as committed to the idea that racial disparities in the rate of contact between the police and civilians *must* reflect officer misbehavior towards minorities, rather than varying propensities for law breaking on the part of different racial groups. During the Bush administration, political appointees to the civil rights division reined in the staff's eagerness to investigate police departments for racial profiling, since the profiling studies routinely served up by the ACLU [American Civil Liberties Union] and other activist organizations were based on laughably bogus methodology. Now that those appointees have left the Justice Department, however, the staff attorneys in the policing section are back in control. And the current assistant attorney general for civil rights, after declaring that civil rights advocacy groups will once again function as the "eyes and ears" of the department, has publicly embraced the advocates' specious methodology for measuring biased law enforcement actions.

The real story behind black student discipline rates is higher levels of violence and misbehavior in school.

Civil rights activists invariably use population data as the benchmark for police activity—measuring the rate of police stops for various racial groups, say, against the proportion of those groups in the local population. If the stop rate for a particular group is higher than its population ratio, the activists charge bias. Such a population benchmark could only be remotely appropriate, however, if racial crime rates were equal. They are not. In Los Angeles, for example, blacks commit 42 percent of all robberies and 34 percent of all felonies, though they are 10 percent of the city's population. Whites commit 5 percent of all robberies and 13 percent of all felonies, though they are 29.4 percent of the city's population. Such crime disparities—which are repeated in every big city—mean that the police cannot focus their resources where crime victims most need them without disproportionate enforcement activity in minority neighborhoods, but it is crime, not race, which determines such police deployment.

This September [2010], Assistant Attorney General for Civil Rights Perez announced a litigation campaign against school districts for so-called "disciplinary profiling"—disciplining black students at a higher rate than white students. He used student population ratios as the benchmark for appropriate rates of student discipline. "The numbers tell the story," he said. "While blacks make up 17 percent of the student population, they are 37 percent of the students penalized by out-of-school suspensions and 43 percent of the students expelled."

Actually, those numbers don't tell the story. The real story behind black student discipline rates is higher levels of violence and misbehavior in school, a reality Perez ignored completely. DOJ's future assessment of police stops and other enforcement actions will likewise inevitably ignore higher rates of black crime.

A Campaign Driven by Politics

DOJ's assertion that the culture of the LAPD is "inimical to race-neutral policing" exploits this same blindness to the facts of crime. The Justice Department has seized on a single exchange between two cops who were caught on tape discussing a profiling complaint brought against a fellow officer. One says: "So what?" The other responds that he "couldn't do [his] job without racially profiling." To the feds, this exchange can have only one meaning: These and other cops are randomly hauling over blacks and Hispanics to harass them. But if the officers were involved in gang enforcement, as almost any officer patrolling in the city's southern and eastern sections will likely at some point be, attention to a suspect's race and ethnicity is unavoidable, since L.A.'s gangs are obsessively self-defined by skin color. Until Los Angeles gangs give up their fealty to racial identity, they can expect police officers trying to protect the public from their lethal activities to take their race and ethnicity into account in identifying them.

> Once the federal attorneys show up in town, for what can be a multiyear fishing expedition through thousands of documents, they rarely disclose to the police department what exactly they are looking for.

The greatest beneficiary of the coming campaign against police departments will be the police monitoring business. Police monitors, paid for by the locality but reporting to a federal court, range from attorneys to former police officials; they are ostensibly jointly selected by the locality and the Justice Department, but repeat business depends on not antagonizing their DOJ backers. The industry has already perfected such fee-generating practices as billing eight hours to summarize a one-hour meeting. Detroit's federal monitor collected from $120,000 to $193,000 a month for her services, for a cool $13 million, which Detroit is now trying to recover after discovering that she consorted with the mayor during her tenure as monitor. The New Jersey State Police spent $36 million to build the racial profiling monitoring system demanded by the Clinton Justice Department and $70 million running it. Oakland's federal monitor pulled in nearly $2 million for her two most recent years overseeing the financially strapped department, which now allocates 35 officers for internal affairs investigations, but only 10 for homicides. Oakland's monitor previously worked for DOJ's pattern or practice section and has just been rehired there, where she can be expected to impose similar staffing priorities on other departments. Now that Assistant Attorney General Perez intends to revive the L.A. model of indefinitely renewable, rigidly prescriptive consent decrees (which Bush officials had tried to streamline), the monitoring business can expect to clean up even further.

There *are* police departments that could benefit from expert advice from actual police professionals on such issues as use of force, but these are unlikely to draw the attention of the Justice Department. Five-man departments in rural areas where the police chief is the mayor's brother-in-law may well have developed questionable habits, such as walloping suspects who talk back to their arresting officers. Perez has said that he wants to pursue "high-impact" cases, however—meaning big-city departments with a national media presence, even if those departments are already permeated by layers of internal and external safeguards against abuse. DOJ's attorneys are homing in on the New York Police Department [NYPD], for example, having recently convened a closed-door session with the city's anti-cop advocates to discuss the multicultural NYPD's alleged failings toward immigrant populations.

The Real Abuse

If the Justice Department were serious about police reform, it would publish its standards for opening a pattern or practice investigation so that police agencies could take preventive action on their own. It has never done so, however, because it has no standards for opening an investigation; the initial recommendation to do so is based on the whims of the staffers, such as: "I feel like going to Seattle and my Google sweep picked up a few articles on the police there" or "My buddy at the NAACP [National Association for the Advancement of Colored People] Legal Defense and Educational Fund called me and asked us to open up an investigation in Des Moines." Once the federal attorneys show up in town, for what can be a multiyear fishing expedition through thousands of documents, they rarely disclose to the police department what exactly they are looking for. Meanwhile, the local press engages in a frenzy of speculation about which racist practices the feds are investigating and pressures the department to cave in to federal control.

While DOJ pursues the phantom of widespread police racism, the real abuse in minority communities gets no attention from the civil rights division. In Los Angeles on Halloween 2010, five-year-old Aaron Shannon Jr. was showing off his Spiderman costume in his family's South-Central backyard when he was fatally shot by two young thugs from the Kitchen Crips gang. Aaron was randomly selected in retaliation for an earlier gang shooting; his family had no known gang ties. DOJ's pattern or practice attorneys had nothing to say about such grotesque violence even as they were rebuking the LAPD for its alleged inadequacies investigating profiling complaints. And if the LAPD had stopped known gang members around the Shannon home after the Halloween homicide in order to seek intelligence about the shooting, every stop the officers made would have been tallied against the department in DOJ's racial profiling calculus, simply because the Kitchen Crips and their rivals are black.

Though reform police chiefs like William Bratton and the NYPD's Ray Kelly have brought crime down to near record lows over the last decade and a half, violence continues to afflict minority communities at astronomically higher levels than white communities. For the last two decades, the public discourse around policing has focused exclusively on alleged police racism to avoid talking about a far more serious and pervasive problem: black crime. If a fraction of the public attention that has been devoted to flushing out supposed police bias had been devoted to stigmatizing criminals and revalorizing the two-parent family, the association between black communities and heavy police presence might have been broken. Instead, the Obama Justice Department promises a further retreat from honesty.

Profiling on Steroids

John F. McManus

John F. McManus is president of the John Birch Society.

As a guest on a radio talkshow, I was asked for my view about SB 1070, the Arizona law featured in headlines across the nation. I said that I approved what the Arizonans had done because the federal government wasn't doing its job and the people were simply demanding relief from the flood of illegal immigrants who had poured into their state.

Talkshow co-host number one was aghast. Asked why, she swiftly offered, "It's profiling!"

Though I could have correctly countered that it isn't profiling, I decided on this occasion to take a different tack. "So you don't like profiling?" I said.

"Not at all," came the reply.

"Then you must be opposed to affirmative action, which is profiling on steroids."

Dead silence ensued, interrupted a moment later by co-host number two who offered, "That's a great argument."

Naming the radio personalities isn't necessary. The point about profiling having caused co-host number one some deep embarrassment, the program moved on to another topic.

Affirmative action is nothing without profiling. It has been enforced by government decrees for decades. In the upside-down world in which we live, it's perhaps not surprising to know that the practice grew from a 1964 law whose wording emphatically barred the practice. That's right; the 1964 Civil Rights Act specifically forbade relying on race, color, religion, sex, or national origin when hiring. Henceforth, employers covered by the act (meaning most throughout the nation) were forbidden to discriminate in any of these manners when hiring, promoting, etc. One of the act's most outspoken promoters, Minnesota's Senator Hubert Humphrey, offered to "start eating the pages one after another" if anyone could show that an employer would have to hire on the basis of skin color, national origin, etc.

But here's what happened: The act spawned creation of the Equal Employment Opportunity Commission, a federal agency given power to interpret the law, encourage compliance, and bring charges against an employer deemed to be in violation. One year later, President Johnson issued Executive Order 11246 mandating the very opposite of what the 1964 act had forbidden. Now, employers were forced to consider the very human attributes they were forbidden to note one year earlier. A madhouse had been erected. Affirmative action, merely talked about for several years, was now law. Its legacy has emphatically heightened race consciousness all across the nation. And Senator Humphrey never ate any of the act's pages.

There's nothing "equal" about employment when affirmative action is in vogue.

There's no doubt that some of the opponents of the 1964 law took their stand because of personal prejudice regarding race. But others, Arizona Senator Barry Goldwater for one, rightly opposed the measure claiming that the federal government had no constitutional authorization to establish hiring practices for an employer. He, too, was called a racist, and any hope to defeat the act died amidst widespread focus on charges of racism. Once enacted, the federal government became a legal force in the workplace on behalf of affirmative action, turning on its head the principle that the law must be color-blind and threatening punishment for anyone who refused to comply. The madness extended to hiring and promotion practices in police and fire departments, colleges and universities, and anywhere else federal dollars have paved the way for federal controls. In time, there wasn't even a need to show dependence on federal dollars in order to dictate to employers whom they could hire and promote.

In 1978, Californian Allan Bakke found himself denied entrance to the University of California Medical School, while 16 less-qualified applicants won admission courtesy of an affirmative action program. Bakke sued and his case went all the way to the Supreme Court, where the justices demonstrated their cowardice by ruling in Bakke's favor (he could now go to the medical school) but refusing to void affirmative action. Racial bitterness continued to grow. Later Supreme Court decisions saw Justices White and Rehnquist fasten the term "racial quotas" to the practice. Even their objections weren't enough to stop it.

Affirmative action has also spawned a form of schizophrenia. It has government agencies, educational institutions, and various other employers who are beholden to federal dollars placing completely contradictory claims within their hiring advertisements. The ads read, "We are an Equal Employment Opportunity Employer/ We Believe in Affirmative Action." There's nothing "equal" about employment when affirmative action is in vogue.

Finally, it must be stressed that Arizona's SB 1070 doesn't call for "profiling" any more than numerous already-existing federal and state law-enforcement practices. Under the Arizona law, law-enforcement officials are required to make a reasonable effort (e.g., asking for an ID that would satisfy the law such as an Arizona driver's license) to determine the immigration status of illegal-alien suspects during "lawful contacts." That's not profiling; it's common sense. Real profiling, the kind featured by affirmative action with all the injustice and bitterness it has brought, continues apace. It should be abolished.

CHAPTER 2

Should Arab Muslims Be Profiled in the War on Terror?

Overview: Perceptions of Racial Profiling by Muslim Americans

Pew Research Center

The Pew Research Center is a nonpartisan think tank that provides information on social issues, public opinion, and demographic trends.

Nearly 10 years after the 9/11 [2001] terrorist attacks, a majority of Muslim Americans (55%) say that it has become more difficult to be a Muslim in the United States, and a sizable minority report having experienced specific instances of mistreatment or discrimination in the past year. A majority also says that Muslims generally are singled out by the U.S. government's terrorism policies. However, reports about these experiences have not increased substantially since 2007 and the number saying it has become more difficult to be Muslim in the U.S. is not significantly larger than it was four years ago.

When asked to name the biggest problems facing Muslims in the United States, most cite negative views about Muslims, discrimination and prejudice, or public misconceptions about Islam. Nonetheless, only 16% of Muslim Americans say that the American people are generally unfriendly toward Muslims, while a large majority (66%) views life for Muslims as better in the U.S. than in most Muslim countries. . . .

The Problems Facing Muslim Americans

Negative views about Muslims, discrimination and ignorance about Islam top the list of the problems Muslim Americans say they face. The most frequently mentioned problem is people's negative views about Muslims (29%), including stereotyping, being viewed as terrorists and distrust. One-in-five (20%) cite discrimination, prejudice and unfair treatment as the biggest problem facing Muslims in this country. Another 15% mention ignorance or misconceptions about Islam.

Far fewer cite religious or cultural problems between Muslims and non-Muslims (7%) and negative media portrayals (5%). Only 4% of Muslim Americans mention jobs or financial problems, issues that have dominated the public's list of most important problems for the past several years. Just 4% say that clashes or disputes within the Muslim community are among the most important problems.

About one-in-six (16%) Muslim Americans say there are no problems facing Muslims living in the United States today.

More than a quarter of Muslim Americans (28%) say that in the past year people have acted as if they were suspicious of them because they were a Muslim, and 22% say that they have been called offensive names. About one-in-five (21%) say they have been singled out by airport security officials because they are Muslim; among those who report having flown in the past year, 36% say they have been singled out by security officials.

More Muslim Americans born in the U.S. than those born elsewhere say they have experienced hostility in the past 12 months.

Another 13% of Muslim Americans say they have been singled out by other law enforcement officials and 6% say they have been physically threatened or attacked. Overall, 43% of Muslim Americans report experiencing at least one of these kinds of acts in the past 12 months. However, reports about these types of experiences have not increased substantially since 2007 (40% said they had experienced at least one of these acts then). Further, nearly as many (37%) say that some-one has expressed support for them in the past year because they are Muslim.

The Perceptions of Particular Muslim Groups

As was the case in 2007, younger Muslims are far more likely to say they have been victims of discrimination or intolerance based on their religion. More than half (56%) of Muslims un-der the age of 30 say they have been treated with suspicion, called offensive names, singled out by law enforcement of some kind or have been physically threatened in the past year. That compares with 35% of Muslim Americans age 30 and older.

More Muslim Americans born in the U.S. than those born elsewhere say they have experienced hostility in the past 12 months (54% vs. 37%). Native-born Muslims who are not Af-rican American were especially likely to report having experi-enced one of the five hostile acts (61%). Among foreign-born Muslims, those born in South Asian countries are more likely than those born in Pakistan to say they have experienced one of these hostile acts in the past year.

Muslims who are highly religious are more likely to say that they have been the target of discrimination or hostile acts in the past year than those who are less religious. Fully 55% of those who are highly committed say this, compared with 38% of those who are less committed.

The Perceptions of Anti-Terrorism Measures

A majority (52%) of Muslim Americans believe the government's anti-terrorism policies single out Muslims for increased surveillance and monitoring, while 34% say they do not think Muslims are singled out. Further, 18% say that be-ing singled out bothers them a lot and an additional 20% say it bothers them some. There has been no increase since 2007 in the percentage of Muslim Americans reporting that Muslims in the U.S. are singled out or that being targeted bothers them.

The general public is more divided on this question—as many say that Muslim Americans are not singled out by the government's anti-terrorism measures (46%) as say that they are (44%). Just a quarter of the public (25%) say they are bothered that Muslims are singled out.

Among Muslim Americans, more men than women say that Muslims are singled out by the government's anti-terrorism policies (57% vs. 47%), but there is no difference in the number saying that they are bothered by being singled out.

As with experiences of suspicion and hostile acts, the belief that government anti-terrorism efforts single out Muslim Americans is far more widespread among native-born Muslim Americans than those born elsewhere. About seven-in-ten (71%) native-born Muslim Americans say that the government singles out Muslims in the U.S. and 57% say this bothers them a lot or some. By comparison, 41% of foreign-born Muslims say this and only 28% say they are bothered by being singled out. There are no significant differences among foreign-born Muslims based on when they came to the U.S. or where they were born.

The Muslim Community and Law Enforcement

Fully 68% of Muslim Americans say that Muslims are cooperating as much as they should with law enforcement agencies investigating extremism in the Muslim American community, while 14% say they are not cooperating enough; 18% do not offer an answer. A majority of Muslim Americans in nearly all demographic groups agree that Muslims are cooperating as much as they should.

More men than women say this (75% vs. 62%). In addition, religiously observant Muslims are more likely than those who are less religious to say that Muslim Americans are cooperating with law enforcement as much as they should (75% vs. 66%).

Airport Security: Let's Profile Muslims

Asra Q. Nomani

Asra Q. Nomani is the author of Standing Alone: An American Woman's Struggle for the Soul of Islam.

For all those holiday travelers negotiating the Transportation Security Administration's [TSA's] new cop-a-feel strategy, there is a difficult solution we need to consider: racial and religious profiling.

The Taboo of Racial Profiling

As an American Muslim, I've come to recognize, sadly, that there is one common denominator defining those who've got their eyes trained on U.S. targets: MANY of them are Muslim—like the Somali-born teenager arrested Friday night [November 26, 2010] for a reported plot to detonate a car bomb at a packed Christmas tree-lighting ceremony in downtown Portland, Oregon.

We have to talk about the taboo topic of profiling because terrorism experts are increasingly recognizing that religious ideology makes terrorist organizations and terrorists more likely to commit heinous crimes against civilians, such as blowing an airliner out of the sky. Certainly, it's not an easy or comfortable conversation but it's one, I believe, we must have.

This past week [November 22, 2010], as part of a debate series sponsored by the New York-based group Intelligence Squared, I argued that U.S. airports should use racial and religious profiling. (Taking the opposite stand was a "debating team" that included the former director of the Department of Homeland Security, Michael Chertoff; Columbia University scholar of Pakistan, Hassan Abbas; and Debra Burlingame, a former flight attendant whose brother was a pilot of one of the planes hijacked on 9/11 [2001].)

I realize that in recent years, profiling has become a dirty word, synonymous with prejudice, racism, and bigotry. But while I believe our risk assessment should not end with religion, race and ethnicity, I believe that it should include these important elements, as part of a "triage" strategy that my debate partner, former CIA [Central Intelligence Agency] case officer Robert Baer, says airports and airliners already do.

A Rational Threat Assessment

Profiling doesn't have to be about discrimination, persecution, or harassment. As my debating partner, conservative columnist Deroy Murdock put it: "We are not arguing that the TSA should send anyone named Mohammad to be waterboarded somewhere between the first-class lounge and the Pizza Hut."

> *Today, the threat has changed, and it is primarily coming from Muslims who embrace al Qaeda's radical brand of Islam.*

And more Americans, it seems, are willing to choose racial and religious profiling as one part of keeping our skies safe. At the beginning of the debate, 37 percent of the audience was for religious and racial profiling, while 33 percent were against and 30 percent were undecided. By the end of the debate, 49 percent of the audience was for religious and racial profiling, 40 percent were against and the rest were undecided, meaning that the motion carried. Of course, this "victory" in a scholarly debate doesn't mean that the motion would necessarily win any broader popularity contests.

In the debate, I said, "Profile me. Profile my family," because, in my eyes, we in the Muslim community have failed to police ourselves. In an online posting of the Intelligence Squared video, a Muslim viewer called me an "Uncle Tom."

But to me, profiling isn't about identity politics but about threat assessment.

According to a terrorism database at the University of Maryland, which documents 60 attacks against airlines and airports between 1970 and 2007, the last year available, suspects in attacks during the 1970s were tied to the Jewish Defense League, the Black Panthers, the Black September, the National Front for the Liberation of Cuba, Jewish Armed Resistance and the Croatian Freedom Fighters, along with a few other groups.

In each of these groups' names was a religious or ethnic dimension. For that time, those were the identities that we needed to assess. Today, the threat has changed, and it is primarily coming from Muslims who embrace al Qaeda's radical brand of Islam.

The Relevance of National Origin and Ethnicity

Data in reports released over the past several months from New York University's Center for Security and the Law; the Congressional Research Service, and the Rand Corporation reveal that over the past decade not only are many defendants in terrorism cases Muslim, but they trace their national or ethnic identity back to specific countries.

According to the Rand study "Would-Be Warriors," the national origins or ethnicities most defendants came from was Pakistan, Somalia, Yemen, Jordan and Egypt, with a handful from the Muslim areas of the Balkans.

To be sure, according to New York University's Center for Security and the Law "Terrorist Trial Report Card," an analysis of terrorism cases prosecuted between 2001 and 2009 reveals that identifying race and ethnicity doesn't mean stereotyping according to country. Among the hundreds of defendants in the study, the largest number held U.S. citizenship. Law enforcement officials familiar with the cases said many of the Americans were ethnically connected to Pakistan, the Palestinian territories, Jordan, Iraq and Egypt. The study, however, didn't look specifically at the ethnicities of the U.S. citizens. According to the study, there were high incidents of cases of passport holders from those countries among the defendants.

Muslim Plots Against Airliners and Airports

The track record of Muslim plots against airliners and airports is clear, starting with the 1989 bombing of Pan Am 103 over Lockerbie, Scotland. After the first World Trade Center attack in 1993, Ramzi Yousef schemed with his uncle, Khalid Sheikh Mohammed, a Muslim of Pakistani Baluchi ethnicity, to blow up 12 jetliners traveling from Asia to the U.S., intending to kill as many as 4,000 people. The plan fell apart in 1995 after a chemical fire caught the attention of police in the Philippines, but a test run had already killed one passenger seated near a nitroglycerin bomb on a Philippine Airlines Flight.

Three years later, Osama bin Laden [al Qaeda terrorist leader] threatened to bring down U.S. and Israeli aircrafts through the International Islamic Front for Fighting Against the Jews and Crusaders, warning the attacks would be "pitiless and violent" and announcing that "the war has begun."

What makes terrorist organizations more lethal is religious ideology. When you combine religion and ethnonationalism, you get a dangerous combination.

"Our response to the barbaric bombardment against Muslims of Afghanistan and Sudan will be ruthless and violent," he said in a statement. "All the Islamic world has mobilized to strike a prominent American or Israeli strategic objective, to blow up their airplanes and to seize them." A declassified CIA memo written in December 1998 warned: "Bin Ladin preparing to hijack U.S. aircraft."

In 1999, we had a "Millennium bomber," targeting Los Angeles International Airport. And, in a case that became very personal to me, on Dec. 24, 1999, a group of Pakistani Muslim militants hijacked an Indian Airlines jet from Kathmandu, Nepal, diverting it to Kandahar, Afghanistan, killing one newlywed passenger. In exchange for the passengers, India released Muslim militants, including a Pakistan-British Muslim militant named Omar Sheikh. Sheikh went on to mastermind the 2002 kidnapping of my friend, *Wall Street Journal* reporter Daniel Pearl, whom Khalid Sheikh Mohammed later confessed to killing.

After the Kathmandu hijacking, we had the 9/11 attacks. And since then, we've had the "Torrance Plotters," the "JFK Airport Plotters," the Glasgow, Scotland, bombers, and the "Transatlantic bombers," all targeting airlines and airports. More recently, there was the attempt by the "underwear bomber," Umar Farouk Abdulmutallab, who last Christmas [2009] attempted to blow up explosives in his underwear—a foiled attack that brought the pat-downs of today. In addition to the Portland plot, most recently, we had the package bomb attempt out of Yemen last month [October 2010].

The Need for Pragmatism

Victor Asal, a political science professor at State University of New York [SUNY] at Albany, and Karl Rethemeyer, a professor of public administration and policy at SUNY at Albany, have studied 395 terrorist organizations in operation between 1998 and 2005, and Asal concludes, "What makes terrorist organizations more lethal is religious ideology. When you combine religion and ethno-nationalism, you get a dangerous combination."

Asal, the son of a Tunisian father, says there hasn't been enough research done for him to take a stand on racial and religious profiling, but favors "behavioral profiling," which assesses risky behavior like buying one-way tickets with cash and flying without checked baggage.

As attorney R. Spencer MacDonald put it in an article in the *Brigham Young University Journal of Public Law*, we can have "rational profiling."

I know this is an issue of great distress to many people. But I believe that we cannot bury our heads in the sand anymore. We have to choose pragmatism over political correctness, and allow U.S. airports and airlines to do religious and racial profiling.

Concerns About Racial Profiling Should Not Inhibit Terrorist Surveillance

Richard A. Epstein

Richard A. Epstein is the Peter and Kirsten Bedford Senior Fellow at the Hoover Institution and the Laurence A. Tisch Professor of Law at New York University Law School.

In the aftermath of the terrorist bombing—no lesser word will do—at the Boston Marathon [April 15, 2013], a major debate has broken out over the proper law enforcement procedures in two key areas: general surveillance and targeted searches. Many insist that a general right to privacy should limit the first, and that concern with racial and ethnic profiling should limit the second. Both of these overinflated concerns should be stoutly resisted.

The Way Forward on Surveillance

The task of unearthing terrorist activities is like looking for a needle in the haystack. Even the best system of oversight and surveillance will turn up an extraordinarily high percentage of false positives, for the simple reason that the odds of any given lead providing useful information, although hard to estimate, may be very small. It takes, therefore, a very large payoff indeed to justify government action in those cases, which is why police surveillance and monitoring should receive high priority only in cases where the risk justifies the large public expenditures and the serious intrusions on privacy of those targeted individuals. At this point, the questions arise of what kind of surveillance should be used, and when and how law enforcement officials can target particular individuals.

The Tsarnaev brothers' attack at the Boston Marathon has brought forth an insistent public call for an increase in surveillance to detect suspicious activities before it is too late. To be sure, there are always technical difficulties in using surveillance devices. But any objection on that ground should be treated solely as means-ends questions, which can in large measure be answered by improved software in such key areas as facial recognition detection. The moral, social, and constitutional objections are sadly misplaced.

Yet, post bombing, intense political opposition has arisen in Massachusetts over the wider use of drones and other surveillance devices at next year's Boston Marathon. Republican Sen. Robert Hedlund of the Massachusetts Legislature has sponsored restrictive legislation on drones with two key provisions. First, the legislation would prohibit the generalized use of drones in Boston, without the explicit prior approval of local governments, including the Boston City Council. Second, the legislation would "prohibit data collection about lawful peaceful activity," which in turn would be backed up by public disclosure of drone use.

Hedlund's stated rationale runs as follows:

It's not surprising that you have law enforcement agencies rushing out to use [the Boston bombing and subsequent manhunt] as pretext to secure additional powers but I think we have to maintain perspective and realize that civil liberties and the protections we're granted under the Constitution and our rights to privacy, to a degree, are nonnegotiable. . . .

You don't want to let a couple of young punks beat us and allow our civil liberties to be completely eroded. I don't fall into the trap that, because of the hysteria, we need to kiss our civil liberties away.

The Role of Government in Preventing Terrorism

Hedlund is dead wrong here—and this is from a writer whose entire career has been devoted to imposing workable and principled limitations on government power.

First, the essential task of government is to preserve the life, liberty, and property of all individuals within its jurisdiction against their forcible destruction by other individuals. Second, a system of *ex post* (after the fact) criminal punishments forms at best only one part of a coherent and comprehensive strategy.

It [is] foolish to elevate privacy—itself a complex notion—to that "nonnegotiable" status under a Constitution that also values the protection of life, liberty, and property.

Compensation after the fact from terrorists is rarely, if ever, available. And even if it should magically materialize, it does not bring dead people back to life or heal the wounded. Criminal sanctions will not deter suicide bombers, nor can they be meted out in proportion to the mayhem that these people cause. Major *ex ante* (before the fact) precautions are imperative to stop the endless loss of life and limb that *ex post* sanctions cannot deter.

Nor is there any "pretext" at work in insisting on greater deterrence. It is easy to pooh pooh a major social threat like terrorism by reducing it to the conduct of "young punks," the very people most likely to engage in violent activity.

The Need for the Collection of Information

Unfortunately, Hedlund compounds his initial error with two further mistakes. His first is constitutional, with the false claim that our rights of privacy under the Constitution are "nonnegotiable." Fortunately, no provision of the United States Constitution requires this rigid and destructive point of view.

The basic command of the Fourth Amendment says that, "The right of the people to be secure in their persons, houses, papers, and effects, against unreasonable searches and seizures, shall not be violated. . . ." For these purposes, the operative term is "unreasonable," which, in light of the weighty interests on all sides of the dispute, requires some public judgment that compares the risks of inaction with those of excessive action. This unavoidable balancing process makes it foolish to elevate privacy—itself a complex notion—to that "nonnegotiable" status under a Constitution that also values the protection of life, liberty, and property.

Second, the last thing needed in these difficult circumstances is a squeamishness about aggressive government action. It is wholly unwise to think that we can turn surveillance devices on and off with the flip of a switch, as Hedlund proposes, and still get the information we need. The correct approach is to do exactly what Hedlund would stop: collect troves of information about the conduct of people in *public* places, which can then be stored for future use.

The key protection of civil liberties lies in the restricted access and use of that information. Unauthorized use is subject to severe penalties and should be invoked to allow for the full collection of the relevant information. Indeed, similar activities have to take place in monitoring the Internet use of suspected terrorists—and similar constraints must apply. The information can be collected and reviewed for limited law enforcement purposes, so long as its unauthorized release or use is subject to heavy criminal sanctions.

One great advantage of this comprehensive approach to surveillance in public places is that it avoids the risk that the surveillance will be conducted in a discriminatory fashion. The collection of information covers everybody who comes to public places. Yet once the information gathered reveals some potential targets, it then justifies closer surveillance of key individuals who can be singled out by their past activities. As the evidence gets stronger, so too does the case for more aggressive law enforcement actions. Whenever possible, these enhanced government activities should be subject to some kind of independent oversight, similar to the surveillance warrants of the FISA [Foreign Intelligence Surveillance Act] courts, which deal with the wiretaps that are in place today.

Reasonable Suspicion and the *Terry* Stop

The need for expedited action also applies to individual decisions of law enforcement personnel operating on suspicion, where the immediacy of the situation makes it difficult, if not impossible, to introduce an added layer of judicial protection.

It surely makes no sense to stop and frisk a proportionate number of white males for no reason.

As far back as 1969, the United States Supreme Court, speaking through Chief Justice Earl Warren in *Terry v. Ohio*, held, after much handwringing, that a police officer did not have to show probable cause in order to stop and frisk a person on public streets. Reasonable suspicion that unlawful activity might happen was all that was needed to justify what are now commonly called "*Terry* stops." Justice John Marshall Harlan tightened the noose still further by noting that whenever the police had enough reason to stop a person, the right to frisking him followed "automatically" given the ever-present risk that the party stopped might be carrying a concealed weapon.

This decision has generated many complaints about racial profiling, an issue that the Warren Court was well aware of at the time. There is no reason to sugarcoat the painful choice. These frisks are honest-to-goodness searches and they can be highly intrusive, covering even intimate body parts where weapons could be concealed. They are also more likely to be conducted in high-crime areas with a disproportionate number of young African-American males. No one can deny the unhappy fact that a huge number of erroneous searches will take place, for which there is, after the fact, no effective remedy at all. Unsuccessful searches yield no evidence that could be rendered inadmissible at trial.

Yet there are no sensible alternatives to the *Terry* rule. It surely makes no sense to stop and frisk a proportionate number of white males for no reason. In addition, it is virtually impossible to construct an intelligent system of *ex post* compensation to redress the large number of low-level harms that undoubtedly occurred when an innocent person was frisked.

Terry was unusually candid in recognizing that it chose the best of a bad lot, by allowing substantial errors in order to protect against yet greater losses. The *Terry* court further hedged its bets by announcing that its ruling applied only to this particular case. But history has not worked out that way. Today reasonable suspicion virtually always justifies the search and the frisk that follows.

The Racial Profiling of Muslims

Clearly, the stakes on ethnic profiling are higher than ever after the Boston Marathon—which makes it all the more important to keep the law in focus. Jonathan Chait recently wrote a short piece in *New York Magazine* entitled: "Profiles in Profiling: From the appalling *New York Post* to the rest of us." He observed:

> The Muslim world has certainly produced more than its share of terrorists. But there is a conceptual fallacy at the root of the nativist paranoia the *Post* (and other elements of the Murdoch media) have eagerly exploited: One cannot infer from the fact that many terrorists are Muslims the conclusion that many Muslims are terrorists.

No one should offer any defense of the irresponsible journalistic sensationalism that Chait rightly attributes to the *Post*. But the defenders of increased surveillance are not making the crude leap of logic with which they are charged. Everyone knows that two propositions are all too true: First, the vast majority of individuals with Muslim background are not terrorists, and, second, a disproportionate number of terrorists are Muslim. It is that last fact that drives the need for further surveillance, notwithstanding the high error rate captured in the first observation.

Indeed, it seems as though the FBI [Federal Bureau of Investigation] had received intelligence from Russian authorities that Zubeidat Tsarnaeva, the mother of the Tsarnaev brothers, was herself a potential terrorist. With that, any doubts about Russian intelligence or the motivations of the brothers falls by the wayside. Law enforcement officials must follow such leads to their bitter end in dealing with the prevention and deterrence of terrorist activities. The quicker public officials shed their reluctance to move decisively in these areas, the safer we all shall be.

Spooked by the Underwear Bomber: Instead of Body Scanners and Ethnic Profiling We Need Patience and Resilience to Tackle Terrorism

Mehdi Hasan

Mehdi Hasan is a contributing writer for the New Statesman, *a political magazine in Great Britain.*

Not long after the attacks of 11 September 2001, I went to hear the Arab-American stand-up comedian Ahmed Ahmed riff on the perils of airport security. "All you white people have it easy," he joked with the crowd. "You guys get to the airport like an hour, two hours before your flight. It takes me a month and a half."

He added: "Security has gotten so bad, I just turn up to the airport in a G-string." Perhaps Ahmed can now leave the G-string at home. In the wake of the foiled Christmas Day terror attack on a US airliner bound for Detroit, in which the Nigerian student Umar Farouk Abdulmutallab concealed a package containing the highly explosive chemical powder PETN in his underwear, hi-tech body scanners are being rolled out in airports—a policy that will cost millions. It may seem the stuff of science fiction but these full-body, millimetre-wave scanners produce "naked" images of passengers and re-move the need for "pat-down" searches.

Hooray! So will we, finally, be safe and secure in the skies? Er, not necessarily. Experts say that the explosive device smuggled on to the plane underneath Abdulmutallab's clothes would not have been detected by body scanners. Ben Wallace, the Conservative MP and former employee of the defence firm QinetiQ, one of the companies developing the scanners for airport use, said trials had shown that they picked up shrapnel and metal but that liquids and some plastics would be missed. "Gordon Brown is grasping at headlines if he thinks buying a couple of scanners will make us safer," he said.

Let me be clear: terrorism is a clear and present danger. But it is not all-pervading, nor is it all-conquering and nor should the minuscule risk of being killed by terrorists keep any of us awake at night.

Terrorism Toolbox

So what does he suggest? "We must now start to ask if national security demands the use of profiling." But does profiling work, either? Is there a readily available racial or ethnic profile of a "terrorist"? Perhaps. But al-Qaeda is nothing if not multicultural, employing a racial diversity policy that would make Harriet Harman proud. Arabs? Mohamed Atta et al. Check. British Pakistanis? Mohammad Sidique Khan et al. Check. Hispanics? José Padilla, the so-called Dirty Bomber. Check. Black people? Richard Reid, the so-called Shoe Bomber and, now, Abdulmutallab, the Underwear Bomber. Check. Caucasians? Adam Gadahn (né Pearlman), the white Californian convert and media spokesman for al-Qaeda. Check. In fact, here's a thought: if a blond, blue-eyed member of al-Qaeda and I both arrived at a US airport to board the same flight, whom do you think the profiler would stop? Him or me?

Terrorism plays on our fears. Fear of the next attack. Fear of being killed. Fear of an unseen enemy. To succumb so easily to such fears and the attendant hysteria and paranoia is to grant an easy victory to the terrorists.

Why not stay calm and not panic? Not overreact? Would this not make more sense? Why do we urge our leaders to promise us absolute or perfect security? Why do we encourage our securocrats as they reach into the terrorism toolbox for ever more intrusive and draconian measures? (Ninety-day detention, anyone? Forty-two days?)

Our manipulated fears can overwhelm us. It matters not a jot that our fears are largely unfounded. Take flying. Air travel remains the safest mode of transportation known to man. Studies show that, each year in the United States, one in 6,800 drivers dies in a car accident. The rate for airline passengers is one in 1.6 million. But as the satirist Bill Maher says: "We don't declare a war on cars."

Let me be clear: terrorism is a clear and present danger. But it is not all-pervading, nor is it all-conquering and nor should the minuscule risk of being killed by terrorists keep any of us awake at night. "Outside of 2001, fewer people have died in America from international terrorism than have drowned in toilets," says John Mueller, a professor at Ohio State University. "Even with the September 11 attacks included in the count, however, the number of Americans killed by international terrorism over the period is not a great deal more than the number killed by lightning."

But our deep-seated fears and anxieties seem to have trumped calm and rational analysis. Terrorism remains a growth industry. In 2003, the US department of homeland security compiled a list of 160 potential terrorist targets across the nation. By the following year, the figure had mushroomed to 28,000; in 2005 it reached 77,000 and, by 2006, the list contained approximately 300,000 targets—including fire hydrants, which were ludicrously labelled a "top vulnerability."

Such threat inflation has crossed the Atlantic. Last year, Lord West, the UK security minister, unveiled plans to protect every public building in Britain against suicide car bombers. Every single public building? This is madness.

Hawks and Doves

So, too, is irresponsible talk of yet another war against yet another Muslim country—this time, the Middle East's poorest state, Yemen, where the Underwear Bomber is believed to have been radicalised. On Fox News, Senator Joe Lieberman, an arch-hawk, proclaimed: "Iraq was yesterday's war. Afghanistan is today's war. If we don't act pre-emptively, Yemen will be tomorrow's war." Lieberman has never come across a Muslim nation he didn't want to bomb or occupy—but what is President Obama's excuse? Or Gordon Brown's? In recent days, both have talked up the threat of Yemen, as well as the threat of international terrorism. They seem to feel compelled to prove that they are not "weak" on national security.

Perhaps they should follow John Kerry, their mutual friend. In an interview during the 2004 election, the senator and former Democrat presidential candidate displayed a much less apocalyptic world-view than our present political leaders. "We have to get back to the place we were, where terrorists are not the focus of our lives, but they're a nuisance. . . . It's something that you continue to fight, but it's not threatening the fabric of your life."

Indeed. There is no scanner, no technology, no security measure that will give us absolute security from terrorism. Nor does terrorism have a military solution. What is required on our part is patience, resilience and a sense of historical perspective. In meetings with ministers and officials across Whitehall, I often see the Second World War poster "Keep Calm and Carry On" on the backs of doors. Our leaders would be wise to heed the advice. Perhaps even adopt it as their New Year resolution. Keep calm. Carry on.

Racial Profiling Is Ineffective in Catching Terrorists

Elahe Izadi

Elahe Izadi is staff correspondent for the National Journal.

The identities of the suspects in the Boston Marathon bombing, which emerged Friday [April 19, 2013], completely negated assumptions born of racial profiling.

Preconceived Bias After a Terrorist Attack

In the wake of the blasts that killed three people and injured more than 175, news organizations and social-media websites picked apart photos of marathon crowds by zeroing in on brown men with backpacks. CNN's John King quoted a law-enforcement source as saying they had a suspect who was "dark-skinned." A Saudi national, first identified as a person of interest, turned out to just be an injured witness. A Moroccan-American teenage track athlete who appeared on a *New York Post* cover under the headline "Feds seek these two pictured at Boston Marathon" now fears for his life.

But the actual bombing suspects, Dzhokhar and Tamerlan Tsarnaev, are ethnic Chechens who have lived in the United States for a decade. Their roots are tied to the Caucasus region—quite literally, they are Caucasian. One attended the same high school that Matt Damon graduated from and was on the wrestling team; the other had boxing ambitions. They both have dark hair and are relatively light-skinned. They are reportedly Muslim, and an unverified YouTube account under the elder brother's name included videos made by Islamic fundamentalists. But it's impossible to determine their ethnicity, much less their nationality, religion, or ideology, simply by looking at them.

Right after the bombings, two main narratives—and corresponding physical profiles—emerged in the media: Was this the work of domestic terrorists, perhaps connected with anti-government groups attempting to make a statement on Patriot's Day? Or were foreign terrorists, linked to some kind of element such as al-Qaida, responsible? While the motives behind the attacks remain unclear, the Tsarnaev brothers don't fit that assumed physical profile of a domestic terrorist (white, American-born men) or a Qaida-linked one (dark-skinned, brown men).

"Until definitive information emerges, it's pointless to speculate on who did or didn't do this. The Oklahoma City bombing was first blamed on men dressed in 'Arab garb,'" Juliette Kayyem, executive director of the Domestic Preparedness Session at Harvard University wrote in the *Boston Globe* the day after the attack. "The thirst for a quick and easy explanation leads everyone astray."

It wasn't until Thursday afternoon that law-enforcement officials released photos of the suspects. Many took to Twitter to proclaim they were white men. But identifying someone's race is difficult, even with a photo.

No religion and no culture or ethnicity has a monopoly on terrorism.

"That preconceived bias was stunted, because you didn't know their background, you didn't know their religious affiliation," says Todd McGhee, a former Massachusetts State Police officer and cofounder of security firm Protecting the Homeland Innovations. "It doesn't matter if you're from a foreign nation, or grew up on Main Street in Boston, Mass. As you looked at the [photos], all you could have said is that they were two men. You could confirm gender, and they were lighter-skinned."

The Uselessness of Racial Profiling

Even if the public had known whether the suspects were white or "dark-skinned," that piece of information was still too vague to be useful—how many men in Boston fall under that description?

While so much is yet unknown, "this is going to be a landmark case study," says McGhee, adding that profiling by race and religion is simply not an effective way of combating terrorism. For one, religious and ethnic communities—crucial to cooperating with law enforcement on terrorism cases—may become alienated. Entire groups of people fall under suspicion, just because of how they look. And others who pose a threat may go unnoticed, such as domestic, homegrown terrorists. "No religion and no culture or ethnicity has a monopoly on terrorism," McGhee says.

The public is better served by being aware of factors such as unusual behavior, McGhee added, or anomalies in something as simple as how someone is walking to whether they are overdressed for an event (as the Tsarnaev brothers appeared to be). Racial profiling is less effective than random sampling for law enforcement looking to catch terrorists, University of Texas statistician William Press has found.

To be sure, federal and Massachusetts authorities have not encouraged racial profiling in how they've handled the case; they simply released photos once they had them. On Wednesday, Massachusetts Gov. Deval Patrick said: "These are times when all kinds of forces sometimes conspire to make people start to think of categories of people in sometimes uncharitable ways. . . . This community will recover and will heal if we turn to each other rather than on each other."

Indeed, in the end, it was assiduous detective work that led to the identification of suspects, not racial profiling.

Racial Profiling in the War on Terror Leads to Dangerous Practices

Center for Human Rights and Global Justice

The Center for Human Rights and Global Justice is a research center within the New York University School of Law that focuses on issues of international human rights law.

The U.S. government's focus on Muslims in counterterrorism operations appears to stem from a series of assumptions about Muslims and terrorism, including the following: that Muslims are more likely to become terrorists; that American Muslims are increasingly being "radicalized" and compelled into committing violence in the name of Islam; and that counterterrorism policies should focus on identifying individuals who hold certain ideologies and exhibit certain behaviors as indicative of "radicalization" in order to stop them before they can act. These assumptions, however, find no support in empirical research. To the contrary, research conducted by a variety of institutions suggests the assumptions in the radicalization theory are wrong. Worse still, government policies relying on these assumptions greatly undermine fundamental human rights.

Conflating Muslims with Terrorists and Terrorism

The first problematic contributing factor to the current situation is the conflation of Muslims with terrorists and terrorism. The popular notion of terrorism has become inextricably

Center for Human Rights and Global Justice, pp. 6–11, 14–15, 17–18 in *Targeted and Entrapped: Manufacturing the "Homegrown Threat" in the United States*. New York: NYU School of Law, 2011. Copyright © 2011 by NYU School of Law. All rights reserved. Reproduced by permission.

linked to Muslims and Islam, due in no small part to a host of government policies targeting Muslims as potential terrorists. There is also evidence to suggest that many law enforcement agencies are trained with materials that construct Muslims as potential terrorists.

Moreover, commentators have noted that the government tends to use criminal terrorism charges in cases involving Muslim defendants charged with violent crimes, but not against non-Muslims charged with similar conduct. Yet, since September 11, 2001, there have been more instances of politically-motivated violence in the U.S. committed by non-Muslims than there have been by individuals claiming to be motivated by Islam.

President Barack Obama, the FBI, the Department of Homeland Security, and the National Counterterrorism Center, have all embraced the theory of radicalization.

In addition, the construction of a terrorist "Other" has conflated notions of race, ethnicity, religion, national origin, gender, and political views, effectively racializing Islam, Muslims, and Muslim religious practice as radically threatening to U.S. national security interests. Muslim men have been constructed as particularly dangerous. "Muslim" and "Arab" are no longer discrete signifiers of religion or race but have been combined—by the media, popular conceptions, and the government's own practices and policies—into a broader category of "Muslim looking people." Muslim cultural and religious practices have also been marked in various ways as indicators of potential terrorist criminality. In turn, law enforcement officers target those who they perceive to look or act like Muslims in terrorism investigations, surveillance, and prosecutions.

The Myth of "Radicalization"

A second explanatory factor is the view that American Muslims are increasingly being "radicalized" into committing violence in the name of Islam. The 2007 NYPD [New York Police Department] report entitled "Radicalization in the West: The Homegrown Threat" has been pivotal in popularizing radicalization theories. Though the theories underlying the report have been criticized as "thinly sourced" and "reductionist," they continue to enjoy support at the highest levels of government. These theories are premised roughly on the notion that [as author and national security commentator Faiza Patel puts it] "the path to terrorism has a fixed trajectory and that each step of the process has specific, identifiable markers." Yet no empirical, social scientific research supports the notion of a "religious conveyer belt" that predictably leads to terrorism. In fact, research suggests that there is no such process that can be identified with any confidence. Equally troubling, the so-called markers of radicalization are over-determinate and focused on Muslim religious practice in fundamentally discriminatory ways.

Nonetheless, the U.S. government has played a role in nurturing the idea that "radicalization" is an identifiable process. In February 2011, under the leadership of Senator Joe Lieberman, the Homeland Security and Governmental Affairs Committee issued a report on the Fort Hood shooting, calling on the National Security Council and Homeland Security Council to develop "a comprehensive national approach to countering homegrown radicalization to violent Islamist extremism." In March 2011, Representative Peter King held a widely criticized Congressional hearing, premised on the assertions that American Muslims are "radicalizing" at an increasing rate; that American Muslims are not doing enough to counter this trend; and that American Muslim communities are not cooperating with law enforcement. The only law enforcement witness called by Representative King rejected the premise of the hearing.

The King hearing is only the most recent manifestation of the government's adoption of the radicalization theory. Elsewhere, President Barack Obama, the FBI [Federal Bureau of Investigation], the Department of Homeland Security, and the National Counterterrorism Center, have all embraced the theory of radicalization.

"Preventative" Policing

A third interrelated factor is law enforcement's shift to a preventative approach to counterterrorism, whereby the government investigates individuals without any evidence of individual wrongdoing. The preventative model assumes that radicalization is an identifiable process, and suggests that it is desirable to investigate and prosecute individuals while they are still in the early stages of "radicalizing" so that they will not develop into full-fledged terrorists. Rather than focusing on the policing of criminal activity, this approach facilitates the criminalization of those who "act Muslim," either through their religious practice, attendance at a mosque, or their expression of political opinions critical of U.S. foreign policy. The use of informants appears to be a core feature of this model of policing terrorism.

A fourth factor—examined in greater detail in the next section—is the use of particular laws and policies that facilitate the preventative model of aggressive policing and prosecution, combined with a concomitant absence of legal or regulatory safeguards. The U.S. government has aggressively used material support statutes, conspiracy or attempt charges, or combinations thereof in terrorism prosecutions, resulting in the criminalization of a range of behaviors that do not seem to be indicative of any intent to commit a violent crime. At the same time, the DOJ [Department of Justice] has expanded its powers and relaxed longstanding safeguards against rights abuses, including, but not limited to, the relaxation of the Attorney General's regulations of the FBI. Moreover, the

DOJ's guidance on racial profiling bans profiling on the basis of race and ethnicity, but does not explicitly ban profiling on the basis of religion or national origin, and creates loopholes for racial profiling in national security and border security contexts.

There are almost no limits placed on when or how law enforcement agencies use informants.

These four factors and trends are mutually reinforcing. Together, they help explain the phenomenon that will be analyzed more closely in this Report—namely, the targeted and abusive use of paid informants in Muslim communities.

The Domestic Legal Framework

Since September 11, 2001, as the FBI has settled into a dual role of an intelligence gathering and law enforcement agency, its authority to collect information has expanded, and its focus, in the counterterrorism context, has shifted to a preventative model. As a result, the FBI seems to increasingly rely on informants, undercover agents, and other forms of surveillance to gather information and, allegedly, to prevent terrorism. Serious questions have been raised about the efficacy and discriminatory nature of these practices, which seem to target Muslim, Arab, South Asian, and Middle Eastern communities as well as activists critical of U.S. foreign policy. In the last few years, the FBI's use of informants, cooperating witnesses, and undercover agents in political and religious spaces has come under increased scrutiny and criticism.

Informants pose a particular set of problems given they work on behalf of law enforcement but are not trained as law enforcement. Moreover, they often work for a government-conferred benefit—say, a reduction in a preexisting criminal sentence or change in immigration status—in addition to fees for providing useful information to law enforcement, creating a dangerous incentive structure.

The following section closely examines the issue of informants by looking at the domestic legal framework governing the use of informants, to wit, the relevant FBI and NYPD guidelines for such activities; and the entrapment defense. As it will reveal, there are almost no limits placed on when or how law enforcement agencies use informants.

From World War II through to the 1970s, the FBI conducted a series of covert domestic operations aimed at various groups considered to be antagonistic to the U.S. government, including through the oft-criticized COINTELPRO program [a secret FBI counterintelligence program started in 1956]. As part of these operations, the FBI systematically surveilled and worked to undermine the "New Left," including individuals thought to be members of the Communist Party, Black and women's liberation struggles, and other groups critical of the U.S. government. The United States Senate Select Committee to Study Governmental Operations with Respect to Intelligence Activities—also known as the Church Committee—found that the FBI relied on "secret informants . . . wiretaps, microphone 'bugs,' surreptitious mail opening, and break ins, [sweeping] in vast amounts of information about the personal lives, views and associations of American citizens" and "conducted a sophisticated vigilante operation aimed squarely at preventing the exercise of First Amendment rights of speech and association, on the theory that preventing the growth of dangerous groups and the propagation of dangerous ideas would protect the national security and deter violence."

Against this background, in 1976, Attorney General Edward Levi promulgated the first Attorney General Guidelines. In the words of Attorney General Levi, these Guidelines "proceed from the proposition that Government monitoring of individuals or groups because they hold unpopular or controversial political views is intolerable in our society." For the first time, the Attorney General placed express limits on the FBI's investigative techniques in order to protect against the types of abuses that marked COINTELPRO.

The Mukasey Guidelines

As documented in a recent study by the Brennan Center for Justice at NYU School of Law [by Emily Berman], over the years, particularly after September 11, 2001, Attorneys General have steadily eroded the Guidelines. Attorney General Michael Mukasey's 2008 Guidelines—currently in effect—reinforced that trend, eviscerating the Guidelines sufficiently as to bring us almost full circle to a pre-Guidelines era.

The Mukasey Guidelines are profoundly troubling in that they allow the FBI to authorize informants and other surveillance techniques without any factual predicate or nexus to suspected criminal conduct. Under these Guidelines, for instance, it is permissible for the FBI to broadly instruct informants to gather names, emails, and phone numbers of particularly devout mosque attendees, without any particular nexus to suspected criminal activity.

> [Current FBI guidelines create] a troubling law enforcement approach of targeting entire communities, rather than policing individuals on the basis of particularized suspicion of criminal activity.

More specifically, (1) the Guidelines authorize the FBI to undertake "assessments" prior to preliminary investigations, in situations where there is no "information or . . . allegation indicating" wrongdoing or a threat to national security; (2) in this assessment stage, the Guidelines permit the FBI to use intrusive investigative techniques such as "recruiting and tasking informants to attend meetings or events surreptitiously"; "questioning people or engaging them in conversation while misrepresenting the agent's true identity"; and, "engaging in definite physical surveillance of homes, offices and individuals"; and (3) the Guidelines "eliminat[e] or reduc[e] many of the requirements for supervisory approval of particular investigative techniques and temporal limits on investigative activity."

The Guidelines are implemented by the FBI's Domestic Investigative Operational Guidelines (DIOGs), which are available to the public only in highly redacted form.

Although heavy redactions prevent a holistic assessment of the DIOGs, it is clear that the DIOGs allow for the FBI to engage in investigative activity "based in part—or even primarily" on "'the exercise of First Amendment rights or on the race, ethnicity, national origin or religion,' of their subject." The DIOGs also allow the FBI to collect "information regarding ethnic and racial behaviors 'reasonably believed to be associated with a particular criminal or terrorist element of an ethnic community'" and "to collect 'the locations of ethnic-oriented businesses and other facilities' (likely including religious facilities such as mosques) because 'members of certain terrorist organizations live and operate primarily within a certain concentrated community of the same ethnicity.'"

The Guidelines and DIOGs work together to authorize extensive surveillance, information-gathering, and "geo-mapping" of Muslim communities, creating a troubling law enforcement approach of targeting entire communities, rather than policing individuals on the basis of particularized suspicion of criminal activity.

In tandem with the Guidelines and DIOGs, the 2003 DOJ Guidance Regarding the Use of Race by Federal Law Enforcement Agencies bans profiling on the basis of race and ethnicity, but does not explicitly ban profiling on the basis of religion or national origin. It also creates loopholes for racial profiling in the national security and border security contexts.

Informants Under the FBI Guidelines

While the Mukasey Guidelines and DIOGs allow the FBI to recruit informants and place them within communities without any suspicion of specific criminal activity, they also authorize informants to engage in activities that would otherwise be illegal, and do not contain an unequivocal ban on entrapment.

The Mukasey Guidelines point to the Attorney General's Guidelines Regarding the Use of FBI Confidential Human Sources—promulgated in 2006 by then-Attorney General Alberto Gonzales—for additional guidance on the use of informants. Both the Mukasey and Gonzales Guidelines explicitly contemplate that informants will be authorized to engage in illegal activity, with limitations only on acts of violence and acts that would be unlawful if performed by an actual FBI agent.

Though the [FBI's] Undercover Operations Guidelines counsel that entrapment should be "avoided," they provide a number of conditions under which "an inducement to an individual to engage in crime is authorized."

Departing from prior sets of guidelines promulgated by [former attorneys general] John Ashcroft and Janet Reno, the Gonzales Guidelines do not require FBI agents to prohibit informants from engaging in entrapment. Whereas prior guidelines prohibited the FBI from permitting an informant to "participate in an act that constitutes an obstruction of justice (e.g. perjury, witness tampering, witness intimidation, entrapment, or the fabrication, alteration, or destruction of evidence)," or to "initiate a plan or strategy to commit a federal, state, or local offense," the Gonzales Guidelines' General Provisions section removed these prohibitions.

The Gonzalez Guidelines address entrapment obliquely. While they require the FBI agent to provide a prospective informant unconditional prohibitions on violence and unlawful gathering of evidence, FBI agents are only required to provide instructions on entrapment "if applicable." The Guidelines do not, however, explain under what conditions these instructions must be given.

In 2005, the DOJ Office of the Inspector General (DOJ OIG) released a report on the FBI's compliance with, among other things, the 2002 Ashcroft Guidelines on FBI Undercover Operations. The Undercover Operations Guidelines include a section regarding entrapment. The language reflects the contours of the entrapment defense—which will be explained in the next section—and a concern about running afoul of the doctrine in court. Though the Undercover Operations Guidelines counsel that entrapment should be "avoided," they provide a number of conditions under which "an inducement to an individual to engage in crime is authorized." In the 2005 DOJ OIG report, the DOJ OIG declined to review the FBI's compliance with the section on entrapment on the grounds that the section "largely addresses authorization issues that we analyzed through examination of the Guidelines' general authorization provisions." Thus, nowhere in this 301-page report is there any review of the issue of entrapment.

A more recent 2010 report by the DOJ OIG on the FBI's investigations of domestic advocacy groups raised similar concerns about the FBI's compliance with its own guidelines. For example, the DOJ OIG reviewed documents that "gave the impression" that the FBI focused on a particular group "as a result of its anti-war views." The DOJ OIG also found "the FBI extended the duration of investigations involving advocacy groups or their members without sufficient basis"; as well as "instances in which the FBI used questionable techniques and improperly collected and retained First Amendment information in FBI files."

The 2005 and 2010 DOJ reports raise concerns about the FBI's compliance with its own permissive guidelines.

Amongst those who have been critical of the FBI's lack of compliance is Mike German, a former FBI domestic counterterrorism agent, currently serving as Senior Policy Counsel at the ACLU [American Civil Liberties Union]. In an interview with CHRGJ [Center for Human Rights and Global Justice], German noted that the 2005 Report "showed that the FBI was out of compliance with its guidelines to an extraordinary extent." German also said that "the Attorney General guidelines are FBI policy. If they're not being followed, that's a signal that something's wrong. The policies were derived from cases where the FBI overreached."

If the government targets somebody based on political advocacy, and can lure a few people into committing bad acts, then a successful prosecution in those cases justifies future targeting of people who are in the same position.

The Entrapment Defense

As the previous section demonstrated, the relevant FBI guidelines provide few checks on an expansive set of available surveillance tools, including informants. However, those indicted after an investigation involving the aggressive use of an informant have recourse to the judicially created entrapment defense. To mount a successful entrapment defense, the defendant must show by a preponderance of the evidence that the government induced him or her to commit the crime charged. If the defendant is successful in proving inducement, the government must prove beyond a reasonable doubt that the defendant was predisposed to commit the crime charged. Although the standards for establishing inducement and predisposition vary across the federal circuits and between states [according to the US Supreme Court in *United States v. Russell* (1973)], "the principal element in the defense of entrapment [is] the defendant's predisposition to commit the crime." Focused on predisposition, the "subjective test" prevails as the general standard in federal courts. The alternative "objective" test focuses on the conduct of the government actors, rather than the mental state of the defendant.

Though it has yet to succeed, the entrapment defense has been raised in a number of federal criminal terrorism cases relying on a paid, undercover informant. The defendants are usually able to demonstrate government inducement by a preponderance of the evidence, shifting the burden to the government to prove beyond a reasonable doubt that the individual defendant was predisposed to commit the crime prior to meeting the informant. But the entrapment defense has consistently failed, because juries have either found that there was no inducement or that the government had proved predisposition beyond a reasonable doubt.

To the extent that the policing and prosecutorial policies relied upon in these cases go unquestioned, these cases will further legitimate the practice of investigating individuals based solely on their religious and political views. As former FBI Agent Mike German notes,

> "If the government targets somebody based on political advocacy, and can lure a few people into committing bad acts, then a successful prosecution in those cases justifies future targeting of people who are in the same position. . . . Whether these cases could survive an entrapment defense is not the relevant question. It's whether it's appropriate for the government to act in a way where they're aggrandizing the nature of the threat. It's just difficult to understand what the legitimate government interest is in these cases."

Between the FBI Guidelines and the entrapment defense, there are effectively no legal protections placed on the government's use of informants. Substantive defenses like entrapment or outrageous government conduct exist, but in particular in the terrorism context, the virtual equation of political and religious viewpoints with predisposition renders the entrapment defense ineffectual.

CHAPTER 3

What Are the Causes and Consequences of Racial Profiling?

Chapter Preface

On the evening of February 26, 2012, seventeen-year-old Trayvon Martin, an African American high school student, was shot and killed by twenty-eight-year-old George Zimmerman, a Hispanic neighborhood watch captain. Martin was walking to his father's fiancée's home in a gated community in Florida when Zimmerman saw him. Zimmerman called 911 to report what he described as suspicious behavior on the part of Martin but, against the advice of the operator, continued to follow the youth. When police arrived at the scene to find an unarmed Martin dead, Zimmerman claimed he shot Martin in self-defense. Zimmerman was not arrested right away because under Florida's Stand Your Ground statute, a person may use deadly force in response to the threat of bodily harm. Zimmerman was ultimately charged with second-degree murder by the state attorney on April 11, 2012, but was found not guilty by a jury in July 2013.

The killing of Martin and the ensuing acquittal resulted in polarized reactions from Americans. A July 2013 *Washington Post*-ABC News poll found that 41 percent of Americans approved of the jury's verdict and 41 percent disapproved, with the rest undecided. However, Americans' views of the case varied drastically along racial lines: whereas 51 percent of white Americans approved of the verdict, only 9 percent of African Americans approved, and less than a quarter of Hispanic Americans agreed with the verdict. Among whites, about one-third thought Zimmerman's shooting of Martin was justified, one-third believed it was unjustified, and another third did not know. Among African Americans, 87 percent believed the shooting by Zimmerman was unjustified, 8 percent did not know, and only 5 percent believed Zimmerman was justified in shooting Martin.

Among those who disapproved of the behavior of Zimmerman and the ensuing verdict, one of the main reasons was the belief that Zimmerman's actions were based on racial profiling, since Martin was unarmed and, indeed, had a right to be walking in the gated community. Of particular concern in this case was Florida's Stand Your Ground law, which some critics say promotes vigilantism. When racial profiling occurs in a state where such a law exists, many worry that young black men will be unfairly targeted by those taking the law into their own hands. And some say that in the case of Trayvon Martin, this is precisely what happened. The authors in the following chapter discuss the Martin case in detail as well as other unforeseen consequences of racial profiling.

Trayvon Martin: Confronting the Problem of Enduring Racism

Doug Bandow

Doug Bandow is a senior fellow at the Cato Institute who specializes in foreign policy and civil liberties issues.

Amerirca is a land of liberty and opportunity, and has admirably served as "a city upon a hill" in the words of Puritan John Winthrop, who led the Massachusetts Bay Colony in the New World. The U.S. continues to attract freedom-seekers from around the world.

Yet America's greatness has come at a cost. Indeed, the nation founded on the principle of individual liberty enshrined slavery in its founding document. Although the U.S. has come far in the 150 years since the great civil war which destroyed that system, racism lives on.

It is a legacy which white Americans like me can never truly understand.

The point is not that America is pervasively racist or uniquely flawed. Nor does the existence of racism justify creating a political spoils system which creates new injustices. However, those who love America the most, and who are most determined to preserve a free society which protects individual liberty, must address America's flaws.

A Controversial Killing

Last month [February 2012] in Sanford City, Florida, a 17-year-old African-American, Trayvon Martin, was walking in a gated community back to his father's girlfriend's home after purchasing a bag of Skittles and can of iced tea at a nearby Seven-Eleven. He had been watching a basketball game and went out to buy a snack. A hispanic neighborhood watch volunteer, George Zimmerman, saw Martin and suspected the latter of criminal activity. A confrontation occurred during which Zimmerman shot and killed the teen. Although Martin was unarmed, the 28-year-old Zimmerman claimed self-defense.

The latter was not charged with any crime [Zimmerman was eventually charged with and acquitted of second-degree murder]. Protests have erupted across Florida and the nation. The Sanford police chief took a leave of absence after a city council vote of no confidence. The state attorney has convened a grand jury, Florida Gov. Rick Scott has appointed a special prosecutor, and the Justice Department has launched an investigation.

It is virtually impossible to dispassionately assess the killing. "He said, she said" controversies are notoriously hard to resolve. There apparently were only two witnesses to the Martin killing: one is dead, while the other has an incentive to lie.

Moreover, no one should be convicted in a media trial. Nor should prosecutions be launched in response to public demonstrations or internet petitions, like that being circulated by Martin's parents on change.org "calling for Zimmerman's prosecution and trial."

Indeed, the protests took an ugly turn with the involvement of the notorious race hustler (and "Reverend") Al Sharpton, who 25 years ago promoted the fraudulent claim of rape by 15-year-old Tawana Brawley. Her claim was discredited and he lost a suit for defamation. At the time he told one of his allies: "We beat this, we will be the biggest niggers in New York." Since then the shameless racial demagogue has raced from controversy to controversy.

However, there is no question that Trayvon Martin would still be alive if he was white.

African-Americans and Criminal Justice

African-Americans long have suffered at the hands of the criminal justice system. Abuses during the Jim Crow era [1876–1965] were legion in the South. Minorities faced racial profiling and discrimination in the North. Despite years of progress, African-Americans remain double victims: most likely to suffer from crimes and most likely to be suspected of committing crimes.

At a meeting held at the Olive Street Baptist Church in Sanford after Martin's killing, local residents detailed violent and sometimes deadly run-ins with law enforcement officials.

John McWhorter, an African-American columnist with the *New York Daily News*, acknowledged America's progress but noted: "police brutality and insensitivity against blacks remain, as I have often argued, the main obstacle to racial healing in this country. I analogize it to a chimney left standing amid the smoking ruins of a house. No one sees the chimney as evidence that the fire never happened. Yet we can't rebuild till we get that chimney torn down."

At a meeting held at the Olive Street Baptist Church in Sanford after Martin's killing, local residents detailed violent and sometimes deadly run-ins with law enforcement officials. The frustration was palpable.

Reported the *Washington Post*: "The stories kept coming, as if it were hoped that they would provide some kind of salve for those who knew and loved Trayvon. People were testifying, a ritual in the black church. The facts about each case were impossible to parse on the spot, and possibly lost forever. But the sentiment behind the stories was unmistakable: Bad things had been done to others with the same promise as Martin. Too many questions had gone unanswered."

What we know about Trayvon Martin's death suggests that he was the victim of racial stereotyping if not animus. From his SUV Zimmerman called 911 to report a "suspicious person." He said that "this guy looks like he's up to no good or he's on drugs or something.... He's got his hand in his waistband.... These assholes always get away.... Shit, he's running." An audio expert reported that Zimmerman also muttered "f***ing punks" under his breath. (The recording is indistinct; other listeners believe Zimmerman said "f***king coons.")

The Killer's Defense

Contrary to the instruction of the 911 operator, Zimmerman apparently shadowed Martin, who called his girlfriend. She reported that Martin "said this man was watching him." Zimmerman got out of his vehicle after which she heard Martin ask: "Why are you following me." Apparently a fistfight ensued, followed by Zimmerman shooting Martin. Other calls came into 911 during which a voice is heard saying "no, no," while one caller reported someone screaming "Help! Help! Help!" In dispute is to whom the voice belonged.

Zimmerman's two 911 calls regarding Martin were his 47th and 48th phone calls to the emergency service, suggesting zealousness or paranoia, or, more likely, a combustible combination of the two.

Zimmerman claimed that Martin attacked him and the police explained their failure to charge the former based on Florida's "Stand Your Ground" self-defense law. The measure grants people the right to fight rather than run, but does not treat every claim as legitimate. The law requires that someone "reasonably believes" use of deadly force "is necessary . . . to prevent death or great bodily harm."

Unfortunately, the police, who previously have been accused of coaching a witness to fulfill the law's terms, appeared to accept Zimmerman's account on faith and ignored standard investigative procedures. Zimmerman had a 110 pound weight advantage over Martin, who carried snacks, not a weapon. Even if Martin started the fight and punched Zimmerman, as claimed by the latter, it is doubtful that would generate a reasonable belief in the threat of "death or great bodily harm."

Moreover, Zimmerman is responsible for the violence. By following the teen, Zimmerman evidently frightened Martin; the latter probably had a far better self-defense claim than Zimmerman. It would be a dubious bootstrap to allow the person who sparked a violent confrontation without cause then to claim to be acting in self-defense. Former Republican state senator, Durell Peaden, who cosponsored the "Stand Your Ground" legislation, argued that when Zimmerman "said 'I'm following him,' he lost his self-defense." Added Peaden: "There's nothing in the Florida law that allows him to follow someone with a damn gun."

Finally, Zimmerman's record was not "squeaky clean" as the police originally reported. He'd been previously arrested for resisting arrest and assaulting a police officer; the charges later were dropped. Zimmerman also had been the subject of several complaints from neighbors about his aggressive tactics while acting on neighborhood watch. Neighbor Frank Taaffe defended Zimmerman, but admitted: "I think he had fed-up issues. He was mad as hell and wasn't going to take it anymore." Zimmerman's two 911 calls regarding Martin were his 47th and 48th phone calls to the emergency service, suggesting zealousness or paranoia, or, more likely, a combustible combination of the two.

The Need to Address Prejudice

All told, Zimmerman apparently was angry and confrontational, suspicious of blacks in his neighborhood, and determined to prevent a potential malefactor from escaping. He followed Martin for no apparent reason other than the fact the latter was an African-American teen. Zimmerman ignored the advice of the 911 operator, caused Martin to fear for his safety, and needlessly created a violent confrontation. Without question Zimmerman exercised bad judgment and made a series of bad decisions; if Martin made a mistake, it was to fight back, but then, he may have reasonably believed that doing so was necessary for his self-defense.

One still should not pronounce Zimmerman guilty of a crime from afar, but it's hard to see how he does not bear some legal culpability. Certainly his conduct deserves official and serious legal review. His case also should be handled like any other. Martin family attorney Benjamin Crump asked: "Do we really believe that if Trayvon Martin would have pulled the trigger, he would not be arrested?" What if a black teen had shot and killed an unarmed white neighborhood watch volunteer in Sanford, Florida? One suspects that to ask the question is to answer it.

The criminal law is no place for a public relations railroad. However, a liberal society governed by the rule of law cannot allow someone to be killed simply because he is a black teenager. It also is important that an entire segment of American society not see itself as disenfranchised, even threatened, by its government.

Trayvon Martin's death is a tragedy for everyone involved. Even if Zimmerman did a bad deed, he likely didn't intend evil. But justice requires holding him responsible for killing Martin, who appears to have been guilty of nothing other than being the wrong race and wrong age in the wrong place at the wrong time.

Thankfully, the era of Jim Crow is over. Unfortunately, the prejudices behind that time have not entirely dissipated. Which means Americans still have work to do.

A Trial in Black and White

Kevin Alexander Gray

Kevin Alexander Gray is the author of The Decline of Black Politics: From Malcolm X to Barack Obama *and* Waiting for Lightning to Strike: The Fundamentals of Black Politics.

A friend asked me if I'd been keeping up with the George Zimmerman trial. My immediate answer was, "Not really. Watching it was really angering me." But when pressed, I had to admit I was avoiding the topic to temper my anger. I also didn't want to try to explain to the white person on the other end of the phone how it feels being black in the USA these days.

Like many others, I believe that Zimmerman is a liar, a racist, and a killer. And I believe that Trayvon Martin had every right to fight for his life with all the strength he could muster. He lost the fight for his life because his killer had a gun, and Martin had only a can of Arizona Iced Tea and a bag of Skittles.

I was a young black boy at one time, and I've raised black boys. I know what they face. I know that white supremacy does take us out at will.

When I was coming up, I would hear a young white man proclaim that he's "free, white, and twenty-one," and that meant the world was his. For black males, the benchmark is "thirty-five and still alive."

So in all honesty, I despise Zimmerman, his supporters, and every racist thing they stand for. I've seen too many victims of raw, racist power wielded by fools.

My friend, knowing me as well as she does, never took my "not really" seriously. After a few moments, I copped to the fact that I had watched most of the trial. And I told her how excruciating it was to hear the defense argue that Zimmerman had a greater right of self-defense than his victim.

That Martin's fists and the concrete sidewalk were his "deadly weapons."

That Martin was basically a "homicidal maniac."

For all Martin knew, Zimmerman could have been a Jeffrey Dahmer-type.

Yet many Zimmerman supporters will only ever see black boys and men as "dope-smoking," "gang-banging" "thugs" and "low-lifes" with no right to exist.

That's what Zimmerman's father, brother, and backers were saying before the start of the trial. They hired attorneys to assert their demand for white privilege. They even found Channa Lloyd, a young, black, attractive female third-year law student to sit behind them in court. Lloyd claimed in an interview that she asked defense attorney Mark O'Mara, "Is George a racist?" to which he responded, "I wouldn't work for him if he was."

Meanwhile, in his closing argument, O'Mara talked about Martin's "fist and the concrete sidewalk" being his weapons while holding up a big chunk of concrete and a picture of a living Martin shirtless.

Then there's Fox News, where it seems that the only thing blacks can do to make them happy is to somehow move to another planet or solar system.

In the months leading up to the trial, Robert Zimmerman Sr., the father of the accused, said, "Racism is flourishing at the insistence of some in the African American community." He called the Congressional Black Caucus "a pathetic, self-serving group of racists . . . advancing their purely racist agenda." And that "all members of Congress should be ashamed of the Congressional Black Caucus, as should be their constituents," adding, "They are truly a disgrace to all Americans." He called NAACP President Benjamin Jealous "a racist" and said his organization "simply promotes racism and hatred for their own, primarily financial, interests" and "without prejudice and racial divide, the NAACP would simply cease to exist."

Like father, like son. Robert Zimmerman Jr., the defendant's brother, sent out a series of racist tweets and photos before the trial. He compared Martin with De'Marquise Elkins, a seventeen-year-old detained in the murder of a Georgia infant. Both pictures feature the young men "flipping the bird" at the camera, with the caption "A picture speaks a thousand words. . . . Any questions?" He also posted several tweets saying that "blacks" are worthy of others' fear, including: "Lib media shld ask if what these2 black teens did 2 a woman&baby is the reason ppl think blacks mightB risky."

Frank Taaffe, outspoken defender of Zimmerman, publicly said, "The stage was already set. It was a perfect storm," and in one CNN interview he offered, "Neighbor-hood (emphasizing 'hood'), that's a great word. . . . We had eight burglaries in our neighborhood, all perpetrated by young black males in the fifteen months prior to Trayvon being shot. . . . You know, there's an old saying that if you plant corn, you get corn." So in Taaffe's white supremacist world, black people should expect to take a bullet for another black person's actions even if there's no connection between them.

Then there's Fox News, where it seems that the only thing blacks can do to make them happy is to somehow move to another planet or solar system, unless they can find a few who are willing to tear down Obama from the right for money. One of their news hosts, Gregg Jarrett, suggested on air that Zimmerman might have been justified in killing Martin because the teen "may have been violent" from smoking marijuana.

Early on in the trial, before Judge Debra Nelson allowed Martin's drug test results into evidence, my wife, who works at one of the big department stores, was in the break room on her job. The news played in the background on the television set as she chitchatted with about five co-workers, all black women of various ages, most either mothers or grandmothers. Into the room comes a middle-aged, fifty-ish white female employee who just started up talking about the trial. There was no invitation for her to strike up a conversation. Nor did she notice whom she was talking to. There was just her arrogant, know-it-all, intrusive whiteness sucking the air out of the room. Or as my wife put it, "She was talking at us."

From the jump, the white woman goes in on Martin saying, "Well you know he smoked that marijuana!" At that point, so I'm told, nobody responded to her. The black women all got up and left the room. And as they got out of the cussing-the-woman-out range, the conversation went:

"White people think they can say and do anything."

"He [Zimmerman] had no business following that boy."

"What's smoking pot got to do with anything?"

"He had no right to shoot that boy."

"I was about to lost my job by giving her a piece of my mind."

"Me, too!"

As I told that story to my friend she became quiet. I joked, didn't that white woman know she was talking to a group of black mothers? Then I mentioned Martin's mother, Sybrina. I went on to say how many blacks are extremely proud of the way she and her ex-husband, Tracy Martin, took the high road throughout this ordeal.

"Dignified" is the word most often used, although I see it as one of those words that means they didn't cuss white folks out. For the most part, the parents have let attorney Benjamin Crump do the attacking. Crump has repeatedly expressed what most blacks feel: If Zimmerman had been killed, Trayvon

Martin would have been drug-tested, immediately jailed without bond, and put on trial for first-degree murder facing the death penalty.

Instead of getting angry at the sight of Zimmerman, I wanted to focus instead on the strength of Trayvon Martin's parents.

I went on to say to my friend that Sybrina Fulton was becoming something of an icon to many black people, much like Mamie Till, the mother of Emmett Till, who died at the hands of racists. I told her that for many blacks, Sybrina represents how they view black mothers and wives. And I said that many black women view themselves going through hell or high water for their kids, as she has done.

In addition, Tracy Martin, though divorced, maintained a close relationship with his son and a respectful relationship with his ex-wife and mother of his child. He wasn't an absentee father. He seemed to be a good parent. But you knew that a white man was going to play the irresponsible black parent game. Kind of like Barack Obama does from time to time, although a Boston College study done a couple of years back revealed—surprisingly to some—that black fathers not living in the same domicile as their children are more likely to have a relationship with their kids than white fathers in similar circumstances.

I found myself posting photos of the parents and their sons on social media throughout the trial. Many others did as well. I did it because I wanted to remind myself and others what the trial was about. And instead of getting angry at the sight of Zimmerman, I wanted to focus instead on the strength of Trayvon Martin's parents. I used words like "respect" and "strength" as captions to cut through efforts to dehumanize and denigrate the family and the slain son.

Zimmerman's defense team wanted words like "gang," "gang-related," "gun," or "drug-related" added to the story because they know that most of the time it strips the accused (who are often black) of their human rights and humanity. They know that if some black kid's face on the news and the word "gun" or "drug" is mentioned, even blacks, unless they're family members, most often don't really care what happens to the kid. The defense's goal was to flip the script and make Martin the accused.

And the defense couldn't put the gun in Martin's hands so they did the next best thing: They tried to bring drugs into the game by advancing the old "Reefer Madness" myth arguing that marijuana makes you violent. Back in the '80s and '90s, usually after a cop shot someone, they'd say the shooting victim was on PCP (angel dust) or crack, and it gave them super-human strength. I haven't seen many super-strong crack heads in my lifetime, but I've seen a lot of them wasting away to little or nothing. I haven't seen all that many super-strong potheads, either.

Painful as it was, I watched defense attorney Don West attempt to paint a prosecution witness, nineteen-year-old Rachel Jeantel, as a stupid liar. Jeantel was on the phone with Martin the night Zimmerman killed him. She was the last person he spoke to. He told Jeantel he was being followed by a "creepy-ass cracker." Her testimony sparked a courtroom, online, and on-television argument and a trumped-up controversy with the premise that Martin calling Zimmerman a "cracker" made Martin the racist.

Don West's daughter Molly posted an Instagram photo, with the family enjoying ice cream after West's contentious and contemptuous cross-examination of Jeantel, accompanied with the description, "We beat stupidity celebration cones. . .#dadkilledit."

In response to the smearing of Jeantel, someone posted online a quote by James Baldwin that read: "It is not the black child's language that is in question, it is not their language that is despised: It is their experience."

CNN devoted airtime to debate "Does cracker = nigger?"

I sardonically laughed as I told my friend, "A cracker cracks the whip that some poor nigger is at the business end of."

Drug-testing Martin after the killing and not testing Zimmerman is just one of the many privileges of racism and white supremacy granted Zimmerman before a single charge was filed against him.

I posted the Last Poet's "Niggers Are Scared of Revolution" to CNN's Don Lemon's Facebook page as an example of one "appropriate" use of the word.

I saw a *New York Times* headline on the case, "Race is an undertone of trial." Undertone? How about, "White supremacy and race privilege reign in America"?

People, such as that headline writer, who substitute the word "race" for "racism" to soften its meaning and meanness always get to me.

Drug-testing Martin after the killing and not testing Zimmerman is just one of the many privileges of racism and white supremacy granted Zimmerman before a single charge was filed against him. I watched trial video of Zimmerman riding in a cop car after the killing and taking the detective on a tour of the crime scene while crafting his lies. No handcuffs. Front seat. I'm thinking, "Wow, they'd never let a black person do such a thing."

I believe the Zimmerman trial is of greater racial and civil significance for blacks than the O. J. Simpson trial.

First of all, there's no epidemic of old black ex-football player movie stars (allegedly) killing their young white wives and their boyfriends.

But there has been a wave of black males killed by whites under "Stand Your Ground" laws. Defendants claiming "stand your ground" as justification for their act of violence against another are more likely to prevail if the victim is black. In Florida, 73 percent of those who killed a black person faced no penalty compared to 59 percent of those who killed a white.

Years ago someone said to me, "White folk believe that most blacks are criminals even if they haven't ever been charged with a crime or haven't done time in jail. They just haven't been caught." As my lawyer friend Efia Nwangaza put it, "To a racist, the average cop, and even the courts, most blacks are either busted or bustable." In a nutshell, racial profiling takes away the "benefit of the doubt."

It's not so hard to imagine that the not-guilty verdict might just give any stranger white man the ammunition (pun intended) or gumption to approach any black man on the street and ask him anything he wants, like: "What are you doing? Where are you going? Why are you here? Let's see some ID!" And what if the black man tells his white inquisitor to "step off"—with or without vulgarities, and the white man responds in a menacing way or tries to detain him or attempts to lay hands on him, and the black fellow fights for his life or does something other than surrender himself to the stranger? How is it that he becomes the criminal and the white man has the right to take his life?

It's reminiscent of slavery and Jim Crow days, when if a white man was walking on a sidewalk and a black person was walking towards him on the same sidewalk, the black person had to step into the ditch or road and give the white man the whole sidewalk to pass. It was a time when blacks had no rights that any white man was bound to respect. But as Vernon Johns, the preacher who preceded Martin Luther King at Dexter Avenue Baptist Church in Montgomery, once said, "You have to have a license to hunt rabbits in the state of Alabama, but niggers are always in season."

I've also spoken with some black folks at various points during this tragedy who are quite open about protecting their children, homes, and themselves. They say, "We got guns too." They aren't gangbangers. Most are working class, homeowners, prior military, rural, many sort of in the vein of Robert Williams, former president of the North Carolina NAACP, who wrote a book called *Negroes with Guns* about self-defense.

What Zimmerman is accused of—and the police are often guilty of—is denying people of color due process and equal treatment with their use of violence.

One young family man, who is not supposed to have a gun or be around one either because he happens to have a couple of drug felonies on his record, said to me: "Look, if it's about protecting myself or my family and I need or have to use a gun, I'd rather be judged by twelve of my peers than carried by six."

One other thing that makes the Zimmerman case far more significant than Simpson is that what Zimmerman is accused of—and the police are often guilty of—is denying people of color due process and equal treatment with their use of violence. And they're often willing to use deadly force even when their lives are not in danger and their victims are unarmed. According to the Malcolm X Grassroots Movement, a black man, woman, or child died at the trigger of law enforcement or "the color of law" every twenty-eight hours in 2012. And in most cases, had the alleged perpetrator been adjudicated and found guilty of a crime the sentence wouldn't have been the death penalty.

As I was talking to some young brothers the other night, they joked that "if Zimmerman had killed a white man, they'd drop the 'white' from the 'white Hispanic' description of him."

Despite my contempt for Zimmerman, he was found not guilty, and the system should protect the rights of the accused whether we like the defendant or not.

Back in the period between the shooting and arrest, former heavy weight boxing champ Mike Tyson (who in 1992 was convicted of raping Desiree Washington, a beauty pageant contestant, and served three years in an Indiana prison) offered a death wish for Zimmerman: "It's a disgrace that man hasn't been dragged out of his house and tied to a car and taken away. That's the only kind of retribution that people like that understand. It's a disgrace that man hasn't been shot yet. Forget about him being arrested—the fact that he hasn't been shot yet is a disgrace. That's how I feel personally about it."

Most of the death threats are probably not serious but a few may be.

One Zimmerman hater wrote: "He has proven that he fears blacks and will kill them because of that fear. He's a danger to black people, and blacks would be within their right to shoot him in self-defense."

I don't support the death penalty by the government or revenge seekers.

To me, the only way Zimmerman could've escaped the contempt and hatred of black people was by saying at the very start, "I messed up, and I'm sorry." And certainly, after the verdict, his attorneys and his family should have had the basic decency to say, "There were no winners today. What happened was a tragedy. And our sympathies go out to Trayvon Martin's family." Instead, the Zimmerman team danced in the end zone—and on Trayvon's grave.

But my anger isn't just about George Zimmerman and his entourage. It's about the repulsive and dangerous swirl of racism that is in the air right now in America. Sean Hannity was typically ugly when he mocked President Obama's thoughtful remark that "Travyon could have been me thirty-five years ago" by saying they both "smoked pot and . . . did a little blow."

My anger is about the racism that still infects our criminal justice system.

Marissa Alexander knows it well. She's the woman in Florida who in 2010 fired warning shots into her wall to try to scare off her abusive husband. She invoked "Stand Your Ground," and she's now doing twenty years behind bars.

So yes, let's definitely work to wipe out the Stand Your Ground laws. But that won't be enough. We need to wipe out racism, too.

The Trayvon Martin case has shaken up a generation of young black men and women. You could see them demonstrating at all the rallies around the country after the verdict. They understood, more viscerally than before, the hostility that greets them every day in America.

Justice for the System: There Is No Institutional Racism in Our Courts and Police Stations

Ian Tuttle

Ian Tuttle is a student at St. John's College and has written articles for the National Review *and* Intercollegiate Review.

"In our criminal justice system, African Americans and whites, for the same crime . . . are arrested at very different rates, are convicted at very different rates, receive very different sentences." That supposed fact has spread far and wide—last year 84 percent of blacks in a *Washington Post*/ABC News poll said that the system treats whites and minorities differently—and has even filtered to the highest ranks: The words quoted above were spoken by one Barack Obama while he was running for president in 2008.

This belief might seem reasonable in the light of a cursory examination of incarceration data. According to the Bureau of Justice Statistics, blacks made up 36 percent of the 1.54 million prisoners in state and federal correctional facilities at the end of 2010, though they made up just 13 percent of the general population. As critics point out ad nauseam, there is a disparity. But why?

Michelle Alexander, a law professor at Ohio State University, blames "the new Jim Crow." Her book by that title argues that the "basic structure of our society" has not changed since the days of segregated water fountains, merely "the language we use to justify it." Because "today it is perfectly legal to discriminate against criminals in nearly all the ways that it was once legal to discriminate against African Americans," our criminal justice system has simply labeled "people of color" "criminals" and perpetuated America's "racial caste."

Invoking Jim Crow—it seems to be part of Al Sharpton's daily routine—is an evocative but problematic comparison, not least because Jim Crow laws were blanket restrictions on innocent Americans, while incarceration is a punishment meted out to criminals because they have committed a crime. Accusations of institutional racism upend debate by presuming the criminal justice system guilty. One can understand why black Americans distrusted the system in the years immediately following the Civil Rights Act, which sought to end an era when blacks were harassed without cause, convicted of exaggerated charges, and condemned to overlong prison terms, and when whites who victimized them were frequently let off, sometimes scot-free. But half a century on? Is there still reason to presume prejudice?

START with the cops.

In his speech to the NAACP national convention in July, Attorney General Eric Holder said that circumstances required his father to explain to him "how, as a young black man, I should interact with the police," and that he recently had the same conversation with his own son. The day before, on MSNBC's Martin Bashir, New York congressman Charles Rangel (D.) declared that "if the police had got a black [George] Zimmerman, the question would be whether they would have beat him to death." Accusations of racial profiling have motivated resistance to New York City's "stop and frisk" measure; more broadly, many blacks claim to be subject to their very own moving violation, "DWB": driving while black.

Anecdotal evidence is cited often, but the data offered as proof of racial profiling are not convincing. In a 2012 paper published in the *Loyola Journal of Public Interest Law*, William Quigley offered a typical example of the poor reasoning in this debate by comparing arrest rates among blacks with their portion of the general population. The ACLU had accused Philadelphia cops of racism 15 years before based on a study with the same flaw. The problem with such racial-profiling statistics, Hoover Institution scholar Thomas Sowell has observed, is that they are "based on blacks as a percentage of the population, rather than blacks as a percentage of the people who do the kinds of things that cause police to stop people and question them." By Quigley's logic, women should account for half of arrests.

Blacks make up just over half of persons stopped [in New York City], but victims describe black assailants in seven out of ten violent crimes—suggesting that blacks are actually under-stopped.

Furthermore, as Heather Mac Donald pointed out in a 2008 essay for *City Journal*, studies of a wide range of crimes have found that victims' descriptions of their assailants line up with arrests, suggesting that people generally are not arrested for crimes committed by people of other races. If cops were racist, a racial imbalance in arrest rates would be more likely to appear in property crimes, where the victim is less likely to be able to give a description. In fact, FBI statistics show a smaller racial disparity in arrest rates for property crime than for violent crime.

New York City's stop-and-frisk program is a good example of racial-profiling alarmism. As New York City police commissioner Ray Kelly has observed, blacks make up just over half of persons stopped, but victims describe black assailants in seven out of ten violent crimes—suggesting that blacks are actually under-stopped. Moreover, the program is much more vigorously applied in high-crime areas, which tend to have higher minority populations. Police go where the crime is.

Robert L. Werling and Patricia A. Cardner presented another relevant finding in a 2013 paper in the *International Journal of Criminology and Sociology*: Minorities are disproportionately likely to call the police, just as they are to use social services generally. This alone would tend to bring police disproportionately to minority areas, but its effect is augmented by the police practice of allocating more resources to areas with more calls for service.

WHAT about at trial? Do prosecutors overcharge minority defendants? And do judges oversentence them?

In 1997 Robert Sampson and Janet Lauritsen published an influential study on this topic in the journal *Crime and Justice*. Reviewing the abundant literature on charging and sentencing available at the time, they found "little evidence that racial disparities result from systematic, overt bias." Yet liberal outfits such as the Sentencing Project and the Center for Constitutional Rights continue to flaunt racial disparities in sentencing as evidence of just such bias. Isolating the influence of race is very difficult given the number of factors that contribute to charging and sentencing decisions. Still, the numbers are worth considering.

A report published in 2012 by the U.S. Commission on Sentencing found that prison sentences for black men were, on average, almost 20 percent longer than those for white men for similar crimes; and the Commission had documented previously that blacks were more likely than whites to be charged with crimes that had mandatory minimum sentences. But the Commission warned against interpreting the numbers as evidence of racial discrimination.

In a working paper released in 2012, law professor Sonja Starr and economics professor Marit Rehavi studied a sample of 58,000 federal cases, including property crimes, violent crimes, and weapons and regulatory offenses. They found that 83 percent of the sentencing disparity between blacks and whites could be explained by differences in criminal record, the arrest offense, gender, age, and location. The disparity that remained was a result of charging differences. Starr and Rehavi say there is no indication that disparate charging is a result of racial discrimination; there are, they note, other relevant factors that might not appear in the data.

From 1980 to 1990 . . . violent crime was a greater contributor to the increase in state-prison populations (which hold the vast majority of prisoners) than was drug crime.

Lauren Shermer, of Widener University, and Brian Johnson, of the University of Maryland, published a study in 2009 that looked at federal charging and found that a defendant's race did not affect U.S. attorneys' decisions to reduce charges. Travis Franklin, of Sam Houston State University, found the same to be true of prosecutors' decisions to drop charges at the state level.

CRITICS of the criminal justice system may concede these numbers but reply that racism exists in the criminal code itself as a result of the war on drugs. Wrote Michelle Alexander in *The Nation*, "The drug war was part of a grand and highly successful Republican Party strategy of using racially coded political appeals on issues of crime and welfare to attract poor and working class white voters who were resentful of, and threatened by, desegregation, busing, and affirmative action." That is, the drug war had nothing to do with an increase in the amount of drugs or a crack crisis in impoverished black communities; it had to do with locking up black people.

But according to political scientist John J. Dilulio Jr., writing in *City Journal*, "the data tell a different story. In 1980 [before the drug war], 46.6 percent of state prisoners and 34.4 percent of federal prisoners were black; by 1990 [four years into it], 48.9 percent of state prisoners and 31.4 percent of federal prisoners were black." Looking at more recent data, Mac Donald noted, "In 2006 blacks were 37.5 percent of the

1,274,600 state prisoners. If you remove drug prisoners from that population, the percentage of black prisoners drops to 37 percent." Not exactly damning evidence that blacks have been disproportionately victimized by drug-law enforcement. Nor was the drug war the main reason for the increase in the number of black prisoners. From 1980 to 1990, when authorities were supposedly swooping down to arrest every teenager on Harlem's streets, violent crime was a greater contributor to the increase in state-prison populations (which hold the vast majority of prisoners) than was drug crime.

A disproportionate share of blacks are in prison because blacks commit a disproportionate share of crimes.

Mandatory minimum federal sentences are also often cited as an indication of the drug war's racism, since they penalize possession of crack cocaine much more severely than possession of powder cocaine, and the former has been more common in black communities. But you could typically avoid the mandatory minimum if you met three conditions: Don't hurt anyone, don't have a gun, and don't lie to the police. In 2006, only 15.4 percent of crack defendants met these conditions, as opposed to nearly half of powder-cocaine defendants. Congress appears to have been justified in viewing crack as the greater problem. The sentencing disparity was in any case dramatically reduced by the Fair Sentencing Act, signed into law by President Obama in 2010.

As for the myth of a white-Republican conspiracy, it was the Congressional Black Caucus that pushed the 1986 Anti-Drug Abuse Act and, two years later, the creation of the Office of National Drug Control Policy administered by a "drug czar"—a term coined, approvingly, by Senator Joe Biden in 1982.

Some allege that the drug war's targeting of blacks has moved to a new drug. In June the ACLU published a study that found that blacks are 3.7 times more likely to be arrested for marijuana possession than whites, despite similar usage rates. This much-touted report, though, does not control for "individual characteristics of each arrest, such as amount of marijuana possessed and the age and criminal history record of the individual arrested," leaving that to "a more scholarly analysis." But those characteristics are crucial to making an accurate determination of the cause of the disparity, which the study does not purport to do; it is "a purely descriptive analysis." Nonetheless Ezekiel Edwards, director of the ACLU's Criminal Law Reform Project and lead author of the report, claims that the study confirms racial profiling—a pronouncement that has, in turn, been propagated by uncurious media. The further questions in need of study are myriad, and the reliable studies are few. Since police are likely to focus more on marijuana sellers than on users, are blacks more likely to sell? Are they more likely to use or sell in the open, rather than secretly? Are they using or selling in areas where there is a greater police presence? If the answers align with those for other kinds of arrests, there is little reason to attribute the racial disparity in marijuana arrests to discrimination.

In the end, the cause of the racial disparity in the criminal justice system is simple: A disproportionate share of blacks are in prison because blacks commit a disproportionate share of crimes. This is what Sampson and Lauritsen concluded a decade and a half ago, and study after study since then has supported their conclusion. According to the latest U.S. Census Bureau data, the white-to-black ratio in the general population is 5.9 to 1. In the prison population as of year-end 2010 it was 1 to 1.18—that is, of the 1.6 million state and federal prisoners, 499,600 were white and 588,000 were black. To match the white-to-black ratio of the general population, the population of black prisoners would have to fall to 84,678— that is, by 85 percent.

Are 85 percent of the current black prison population victims of racism?

None of this is to deny the existence of racist cops, racist attorneys, racist jurors, and racist judges. But unlike that of the Jim Crow era, any racism in the criminal justice system today cannot be shown to be institutional, and it is likely to be corrected by the many checks within the system.

As accusations of entrenched prejudice extending from the squad car to the jury box persist, those who know the facts can only continue to present their case and do their best to get the evidence a fair trial.

Racial Profiling in America Is Part of Systemic Racism

Gary Younge

Gary Younge is the Alfred Knobler Journalism Fellow at the Nation Institute, the New York correspondent for the Guardian *newspaper, and the author of* The Speech: The Story Behind Dr. Martin Luther King Jr.'s Dream.

Not long after George Zimmerman was charged [in April 2012] with killing Trayvon Martin [on February 26, 2012], his wife, Shellie, called him in jail with an update on the money flooding into his PayPal account.

"After this is all over," Shellie later told him, "you're going to be able to just have a great life."

The Profile of an Individual

But in the nearly three months since his acquittal [in July 2013], the Zimmermans' life hasn't looked so great. It's been unraveling in a style and at a pace that, in different circumstances, might have one day earned them a reality show. But Keeping Up With the Zimmermans is no joke. Shellie, who admitted to perjury for lying about not knowing how much money George had before the trial, has since filed for divorce, accusing him of having an affair with his ex-fiancée—the same one who filed a domestic violence report against him in 2005.

Within the past six weeks, Zimmerman has been caught speeding twice and has been taken into custody after punch-

Gary Younge, "George Zimmerman's Way Is the American Way," *The Nation*, October 7, 2013. Reprinted with permission from the October 7, 2013 issue of The Nation. For subscription information, call 1-800-333-8536. Portions of each week's Nation magazine can be accessed at http://www.thenation.com.

ing his father-in-law in the nose and threatening to shoot him and Shellie. Zimmerman claims they were the aggressors.

"He's in his car and he continually has his hand on his gun and he keeps saying step closer . . . and he's gonna shoot us," Shellie told the 911 operator. "I don't know what he's capable of."

But we do. The violence, recklessness, inadequacy and preening self-regard exhibited over the last few months by Zimmerman are precisely the kind of attributes that would lead an armed man to chase an unarmed boy, confront him, shoot him dead and then claim self-defense. The police chief in the city where he now lives agreed he was "a ticking time bomb" and a "Sandy Hook [referring to the December 2012 massacre at Sandy Hook Elementary School in Newtown, Connecticut] waiting to happen."

But the more we delve into George Zimmerman's psychology, the further we stray from the politics that makes his slaying of Trayvon important and his acquittal outrageous. For the key problem with Zimmerman is not that he's a bad person.

Zimmerman's assumptions about Trayvon are not simply the product of a sick mind but of a sick society.

The Problem of Racism

Racism is not about bad manners, but a system of privilege, discrimination and brutality embedded in American society and across its institutions that operates to exclude, demean and restrict. It does not need a pointy hood and burning cross to work, or mean-spirited people to ensure it runs smoothly. Likewise, its victims do not need to lead lives of unblemished innocence to be worthy of defense. Racism finds them guilty of being black—the rest is gravy.

There is a crucial distinction here between the legal and the political. Legally, speculation as to Zimmerman's intentions that night are central to the case. But politically, to dwell on his state of mind is to enter a fruitless discussion about who he is. As Jay Smooth, in his great blog "How to Tell People They Sound Racist," points out, you can't win that discussion because nothing can be proven and everything is subjective. Worse still, you are drawn away from talking about what kind of racist society America is, and into talking about what kind of person Zimmerman is. Juror B-37 insisted his "heart was in the right place," while Shellie Zimmerman argued that racial profiling is "just not his way." We can't speak with any authority about his heart or his way, but it's incumbent on us to continue having a meaningful discussion about what he did. For in his pursuit, apprehension and killing of Trayvon, what we saw was a freelance stop-and-frisk that turned into a stop-and-shoot. Zimmerman didn't know Trayvon, but he assumed he was "a punk."

Just a few months before Zimmerman's trial, these very assumptions were tested in a Manhattan courtroom. According to the Center for Constitutional Rights, which brought the class action lawsuit over stop-and-frisk, nearly nine out of ten stopped-and-frisked New Yorkers were innocent of any violation, let alone a crime. There have been more than 5 million such stops in the past decade, mostly of black and Latino youth. I'm sure all of these policemen had loved ones who would swear to their good hearts and gentle manners. Most could produce a friend of color who could testify to their inherent decency. Some were black or Latino themselves. It doesn't matter. The problem isn't as much systematic as systemic.

The American Way

Black men in America are more likely to be stopped, searched, arrested, convicted and executed and less likely to be educated or employed than any other group. Almost one in ten is behind bars. Compound this with lax gun laws, vigilante statutes like "stand your ground," racial disparities in wealth and income, and segregation, and the system is set up for entirely this kind of incident and this kind of acquittal. Zimmerman's assumptions about Trayvon are not simply the product of a sick mind but of a sick society. This excuses nothing that he did as an individual, but it finds a more substantial explanation for his actions in a defective pattern rather than a defective personality.

The Zimmerman verdict came down the opening weekend of *Fruitvale Station*, a film about Oscar Grant's shooting at the hands of Oakland police. Six weeks earlier, Darius Simmons, 13, was shot dead in front of his mother by a 75-year-old neighbor who accused him of burgling his home. Two months after Zimmerman's verdict, Jonathan Ferrell was shot dead by police after seeking help following a car crash. When he knocked on a stranger's door asking for help, the homeowner didn't call the ambulance, but hit the panic button.

There are only so many isolated incidents you can talk about before you have to start talking about a trend. We don't need to pontificate about what kind of person Zimmerman is because we know what kind of country America is. Racial profiling—and its lethal consequences—may or may not be "his way" but it's the American way.

We Are All Juan Williams: Associating Minorities with Crime Is Irrational, Unjust, and Completely Normal

Shankar Vedantam

Shankar Vedantam is a science correspondent for NPR (National Public Radio) and author of The Hidden Brain: How Our Unconscious Minds Elect Presidents, Control Markets, Wage Wars, and Save Our Lives.

[Journalist] Juan Williams told [TV host] Bill O'Reilly that he gets nervous at airports when he sees Muslims. For this, Williams has been roundly denounced as a bigot. But Williams' association between innocent Muslims and the perpetrators of the 9-11 [2001] attacks was less about bigotry—at least, bigotry conventionally defined—than about his mind working normally. To live in America in the post-9/11 age and not have at least some associations between Muslims and terrorism means something is wrong with you.

A Normal Aspect of Brain Functioning

I am not suggesting that associating ordinary Muslims with terrorists is either rational or right. It's neither. But the association arises via a normal aspect of brain functioning, which is precisely why so many people entertain such beliefs—and why those beliefs have proved so resistant to challenge.

The left is wrong to wish the association away only by pointing out how unfair it is, because that denies the reality of how our minds work. The right is wrong to believe the association must be accurate merely because it is widespread.

It may be helpful to see how the bias works in a less incendiary context than racial profiling and terrorism. Let's say you have an upset stomach on the morning before you take a flight. (This example comes straight from my book.) You don't make much of it because you know that things that occur together are not necessarily related. Now let's say you have a second upset stomach the following week, right before you have to take another flight. Your conscious mind might still say, "coincidences happen," but now a part of your mind starts to think that flying brings on upset stomachs.

The Linking of Unusual Events

What's interesting about this is not that our unconscious minds confuse correlation with causation—our conscious minds do that all the time, too. What's interesting is that the events our unconscious minds link together are only the unusual ones. On both days you had upset stomachs, a newspaper may have been delivered to your door, but you don't associate newspaper delivery with your upset stomach.

These automatic associations make evolutionary sense. If one of our ancestors was wandering in a desert and came by a snake curled up next to the only tree on the landscape, her mind would connect not just that tree with that snake, but all trees with snakes. Illusory correlations are all about seeking out group patterns based on rare individual incidents: all trees and snakes and all flights with stomach upsets, rather than that one tree and that one snake, or that one flight and that one stomach upset. Scientists say correlation isn't causation, but, from an evolutionary point of view, if the snake-tree link is wrong, all that would happen is our ancestor would avoid all trees in the future. If the link was real and she failed to see it, she could get herself killed. Our ancestors constantly drew conclusions about their environment based on limited evidence. Waiting for causative evidence could have proved costly, whereas extrapolating causation from correlation was less costly.

In every country on earth, you can find minority groups that get tagged with various pathologies for no better reason than that the pathologies are unusual and the minorities are minorities.

The terrorist attacks of 9/11 were unusual. (Even if you take all the terrorist attacks in the world, they are still unusual.) In seeking explanations for those events, our minds are drawn to other unusual things linked to them—especially at the group level. When members of a minority group are associated with a series of unusual incidents, our minds inflate the connection between the two. As with the snake and the tree, our association is not limited to the particular members of the minority group but all members of the group.

Juan Williams pointed out on Fox [News Channel] that we do not associate Timothy McVeigh and the rude people who protest about homosexuality at military funerals with Christianity. But he didn't understand why our minds fail to make that connection. Illusory correlations disproportionately afflict minorities because, in making associations, we mainly link unlikely events. Whites and Christians are not minorities; they are like the newspaper delivered to our front door every day. We do not associate McVeigh with Christians any more than we associate our upset stomach with the newspaper.

Muslims are only the latest victim of illusory correlations in the United States. African-Americans have long suffered the same bias when it comes to crime. In every country on earth, you can find minority groups that get tagged with various pathologies for no better reason than that the pathologies are unusual and the minorities are minorities.

The Mind's Propensity to Form Links

Whenever people who strongly believe in illusory correlations are challenged about their beliefs, they invariably find ways to make their behavior seem conscious and rational. Those who would explicitly link all Muslims with terrorism might point to evidence showing that some Muslims say they want to wage a war against the West, that a large preponderance of terrorist attacks today are carried out by Muslims, and so on. This is similar to our longstanding national narrative about blacks and crime.

But even if blacks and whites do not commit crimes at the same rate, and even if Muslims are overrepresented among today's terrorists, our mental associations between these groups and heinous events are made disproportionately large by the unconscious bias that causes us to form links between unusual events and minorities.

A rational Bill O'Reilly should be much more exercised about asteroids striking Earth, or dying from dog bites, than about Muslims being terrorists.

The researchers Franklin D. Gilliam Jr., Shanto Iyengar, Adam Simon, and Oliver Wright once conducted a simple experiment that demonstrated how illusory correlations work: They showed volunteers a television news program that featured a violent crime. Some volunteers were shown a white suspect, while others were shown a black suspect, but everything else about the program remained identical. The volunteers who saw the black face were more likely to blame blacks as a whole for rising crime than the volunteers who saw the white suspect were to blame whites for rising crime. (The volunteers in the white scenario blamed that individual suspect for the crime.) The bias showed up among white as well as black volunteers.

People in Thailand will associate white American tourists with pedophilia even though many more acts of pedophilia are committed by Thais. But white Americans are a minority in Thailand, as are acts of pedophilia. So you will hear Thai people shout until they are blue in the face about individual anecdotes showing white Americans who are pedophiles. (The same is true of gay men and pedophilia in the United States.)

The Association Between Muslims and Terrorists

When it comes to our associations between Muslims and terrorism, commentators on the left are being wishful when they imagine we can rid our minds of false associations merely by holding consciously egalitarian views. Commentators on the right are doing something much more dangerous, however: They are rationalizing and justifying a mental process that is fundamentally not rational and deeply unjust.

If you know there are 1 billion Muslims on our planet (low estimate) and you've heard of 1,000 incidents where Muslims carried out terrorist attacks (an exaggerated number), and terrorist sympathies were (improbably) distributed evenly across the world, the odds that a particular Muslim is a terrorist are about 1 in a million. A rational Bill O'Reilly should be much more exercised about asteroids striking Earth, or dying from dog bites, than about Muslims being terrorists.

The fact that so many of us subscribe to illusory correlations can be blamed on our unconscious minds. The fact so few of us challenge our unconscious minds? That's on us.

Racial Profiling May Increase Crime Among Those Not Profiled

Eric Horowitz

Eric Horowitz is a social science writer and education researcher.

A confluence of unrelated events—New York City's [NYC] mayoral election, NYC Police Commish Ray Kelly being floated as a potential Dept. of Homeland Security Chief, a big judicial ruling—have put stop-and-frisk policies under the microscope.

The Effect of Stop-and-Frisk Policies

Much has been written about the negative impact such policies have on Black and Hispanic communities. And much has been written about the constitutionality of randomly searching people on the street. But how does stop-and-frisk affect those who aren't being stopped or frisked. Or as they like to say in the halls of the Capitol, "how does this policy affect White people?"

A new study set to be published in *Law and Human Behavior* suggests that racial profiling makes white people more likely to engage in illicit behavior. The study, which was led by Georgia Southern's Amy Hackney, used an experimental setting in which groups composed of White and Black students were tested on their ability to complete difficult anagrams. Students had access to an answer key and graded their own exams, and so they had ample opportunity to cheat. The manipulation occurred right before the test began, when the experimenter stared directly at two students and explained that cheating would not be tolerated. He then asked both students to move their desks closer to the front of the room. In one condition the two students were Black. In another condition the two students were White. A third condition with no profiling functioned as a control.

Examining two types of students (White and Black) in three different conditions produced six measurements of cheating frequency.

They were all fairly similar, but there was one exception. White students cheated more when they saw Black students being profiled. They cheated at a higher rate than black students who saw Whites profiled, Whites who saw Whites profiled, or either group when there was no profiling.

> We theorized that heightened surveillance of members of a minority group would increase illicit activity in the majority group—that it would have a reverse deterrent effect. We found that White participants in the Black-profiled condition cheated more than participants in any other condition. Although cheating on a test of this sort is not a crime, it is a dishonest behavior that is a particularly serious transgression in academic settings. These results indicate that racial profiling could increase crime among nonprofiled groups, having a counterproductive effect.

The Feeling of Impunity

Hackney reasoned that seeing others get profiled increases your feeling of impunity, but there doesn't have to be an overwhelming feeling of impunity for profiling to affect nonprofiled groups. Even if people aren't thinking, "I'm white, therefore I can get away with this," they still may come to believe their actions are more justifiable. Eventually a bar fight becomes mischief rather than assault, or stealing that piece of art your friend will love is an act of kindness rather than breaking and entering. Perhaps you manage to rationalize stealing a marble rye from an old lady.

When talking about stop-and-frisk it's easy to get caught up in the intricacies of crime statistics and constitutional law. But it's important to remember that these policies influence social norms and the way people see themselves. When people of different races are treated differently based on conjecture—even when that conjecture is based on cursory data—it has an impact on the way people see the world. Ending stop-and-frisk might not fix our culture of white crime, but it would create an image of society that's marginally more conducive to social progress.

CHAPTER 4

What Should Be Done About Racial Profiling?

Chapter Preface

In early 2001, President George W. Bush instructed the attorney general to review the use of race as a factor in federal law enforcement. In 2003, the US Department of Justice issued its "Guidance Regarding the Use of Race by Federal Law Enforcement Agencies." The guidance banned racial profiling with some exceptions. In 2014, the Justice Department reported that it was expanding its definition of racial profiling from these 2003 guidelines.

The 2003 guidelines put forth two standards to guide federal law enforcement authorities. The first bans the use of race or ethnicity in making any routine or spontaneous law enforcement decisions: "Federal law enforcement officers may not use race or ethnicity to any degree, except that officers may rely on race and ethnicity in a specific suspect description." Furthermore, within a specific investigation, "federal law enforcement officers may consider race and ethnicity only to the extent that there is trustworthy information, relevant to the locality or time frame, that links persons of a particular race or ethnicity to an identified criminal incident, scheme, or organization."

The 2003 guidelines did not change federal policy with respect to national security, noting that to prevent threats to national security or air transportation security federal law enforcement officers "may not consider race or ethnicity except to the extent permitted by the Constitution and laws of the United States." The guidelines note that although this exception does not allow "invidious discrimination" there are exceptional cases where law enforcement personnel may be justified in profiling by race or ethnicity in order to protect national security interests.

In January 2014, Matt Apuzzo of the *New York Times* reported that the Justice Department was set to expand its definition of racial profiling "to prohibit federal agents from considering religion, national origin, gender and sexual orientation in their investigations." Whether or not the exception for national security will remain intact is unknown. The federal guidelines only apply to law enforcement practices by federal authorities. However, such guidelines are frequently copied by state and local law enforcement agencies.

There is widespread disagreement, as the viewpoints of this chapter illustrate, regarding legislation and guidelines affecting racial profiling. Whether or not existing guidelines are helping or hurting law enforcement, and whether or not further legislation is needed, are open to debate.

Racism Against Young African American Men Needs to Be Addressed

Barack Obama

Barack Obama is the forty-fourth president of the United States.

The reason I actually wanted to come out today is not to take questions, but to speak to an issue that obviously has gotten a lot of attention over the course of the last week—the issue of the Trayvon Martin ruling [July 13, 2013, the acquittal of George Zimmerman in the murder of Martin]. I gave a preliminary statement right after the ruling on Sunday. But watching the debate over the course of the last week, I thought it might be useful for me to expand on my thoughts a little bit.

First of all, I want to make sure that, once again, I send my thoughts and prayers, as well as Michelle's, to the family of Trayvon Martin, and to remark on the incredible grace and dignity with which they've dealt with the entire situation. I can only imagine what they're going through, and it's remarkable how they've handled it.

The Context of the Ruling

The second thing I want to say is to reiterate what I said on Sunday, which is there's going to be a lot of arguments about the legal issues in the case—I'll let all the legal analysts and talking heads address those issues. The judge conducted the trial in a professional manner. The prosecution and the defense made their arguments. The juries were properly instructed that in a case such as this reasonable doubt was rel-

Barack Obama, "Remarks by the President on Trayvon Martin," The White House, Office of the Press Secretary, July 19, 2013.

evant, and they rendered a verdict. And once the jury has spoken, that's how our system works. But I did want to just talk a little bit about context and how people have responded to it and how people are feeling.

You know, when Trayvon Martin was first shot I said that this could have been my son. Another way of saying that is Trayvon Martin could have been me 35 years ago. And when you think about why, in the African American community at least, there's a lot of pain around what happened here, I think it's important to recognize that the African American community is looking at this issue through a set of experiences and a history that doesn't go away.

There are very few African American men in this country who haven't had the experience of being followed when they were shopping in a department store. That includes me. There are very few African American men who haven't had the experience of walking across the street and hearing the locks click on the doors of cars. That happens to me—at least before I was a senator. There are very few African Americans who haven't had the experience of getting on an elevator and a woman clutching her purse nervously and holding her breath until she had a chance to get off. That happens often.

[There's] a sense that if a white male teen was involved in the same kind of scenario, that, from top to bottom, both the outcome and the aftermath might have been different.

The Context of Black Crime

And I don't want to exaggerate this, but those sets of experiences inform how the African American community interprets what happened one night in Florida. And it's inescapable for people to bring those experiences to bear. The African American community is also knowledgeable that there is a history of

racial disparities in the application of our criminal laws—
everything from the death penalty to enforcement of our drug
laws. And that ends up having an impact in terms of how
people interpret the case.

Now, this isn't to say that the African American community is naïve about the fact that African American young men
are disproportionately involved in the criminal justice system;
that they're disproportionately both victims and perpetrators
of violence. It's not to make excuses for that fact—although
black folks do interpret the reasons for that in a historical
context. They understand that some of the violence that takes
place in poor black neighborhoods around the country is
born out of a very violent past in this country, and that the
poverty and dysfunction that we see in those communities can
be traced to a very difficult history.

And so the fact that sometimes that's unacknowledged
adds to the frustration. And the fact that a lot of African
American boys are painted with a broad brush and the excuse
is given, well, there are these statistics out there that show that
African American boys are more violent—using that as an excuse to then see sons treated differently causes pain.

I think the African American community is also not naïve
in understanding that, statistically, somebody like Trayvon
Martin was statistically more likely to be shot by a peer than
he was by somebody else. So folks understand the challenges
that exist for African American boys. But they get frustrated, I
think, if they feel that there's no context for it and that context is being denied. And that all contributes I think to a sense
that if a white male teen was involved in the same kind of
scenario, that, from top to bottom, both the outcome and the
aftermath might have been different.

New Training for Law Enforcement

Now, the question for me at least, and I think for a lot of
folks, is where do we take this? How do we learn some lessons

from this and move in a positive direction? I think it's understandable that there have been demonstrations and vigils and protests, and some of that stuff is just going to have to work its way through, as long as it remains nonviolent. If I see any violence, then I will remind folks that that dishonors what happened to Trayvon Martin and his family. But beyond protests or vigils, the question is, are there some concrete things that we might be able to do.

I know that [US Attorney General] Eric Holder is reviewing what happened down there, but I think it's important for people to have some clear expectations here. Traditionally, these are issues of state and local government, the criminal code. And law enforcement is traditionally done at the state and local levels, not at the federal levels.

That doesn't mean, though, that as a nation we can't do some things that I think would be productive. So let me just give a couple of specifics that I'm still bouncing around with my staff, so we're not rolling out some five-point plan, but some areas where I think all of us could potentially focus.

I think it would be useful for us to examine some state and local laws to see if . . . they are designed in such a way that they may encourage the kinds of altercations and confrontations and tragedies that we saw in the Florida case.

Number one, precisely because law enforcement is often determined at the state and local level, I think it would be productive for the Justice Department, governors, mayors to work with law enforcement about training at the state and local levels in order to reduce the kind of mistrust in the system that sometimes currently exists.

When I was in Illinois, I passed racial profiling legislation, and it actually did just two simple things. One, it collected data on traffic stops and the race of the person who was stopped. But the other thing was it resourced us training police departments across the state on how to think about potential racial bias and ways to further professionalize what they were doing.

And initially, the police departments across the state were resistant, but actually they came to recognize that if it was done in a fair, straightforward way that it would allow them to do their jobs better and communities would have more confidence in them and, in turn, be more helpful in applying the law. And obviously, law enforcement has got a very tough job.

So that's one area where I think there are a lot of resources and best practices that could be brought to bear if state and local governments are receptive. And I think a lot of them would be. And let's figure out are there ways for us to push out that kind of training.

Stand Your Ground Laws

Along the same lines, I think it would be useful for us to examine some state and local laws to see if it—if they are designed in such a way that they may encourage the kinds of altercations and confrontations and tragedies that we saw in the Florida case, rather than diffuse potential altercations.

I know that there's been commentary about the fact that the "stand your ground" laws in Florida were not used as a defense in the case. On the other hand, if we're sending a message as a society in our communities that someone who is armed potentially has the right to use those firearms even if there's a way for them to exit from a situation, is that really going to be contributing to the kind of peace and security and order that we'd like to see?

And for those who resist that idea that we should think about something like these "stand your ground" laws, I'd just ask people to consider, if Trayvon Martin was of age and armed, could he have stood his ground on that sidewalk? And do we actually think that he would have been justified in shooting Mr. Zimmerman who had followed him in a car because he felt threatened? And if the answer to that question is at least ambiguous, then it seems to me that we might want to examine those kinds of laws.

A More Perfect Union

Number three—and this is a long-term project—we need to spend some time in thinking about how do we bolster and reinforce our African American boys. And this is something that Michelle and I talk a lot about. There are a lot of kids out there who need help who are getting a lot of negative reinforcement. And is there more that we can do to give them the sense that their country cares about them and values them and is willing to invest in them?

> *Those of us in authority should be doing everything we can to encourage the better angels of our nature, as opposed to using these episodes to heighten divisions.*

I'm not naïve about the prospects of some grand, new federal program. I'm not sure that that's what we're talking about here. But I do recognize that as President, I've got some convening power, and there are a lot of good programs that are being done across the country on this front. And for us to be able to gather together business leaders and local elected officials and clergy and celebrities and athletes, and figure out how are we doing a better job helping young African American men feel that they're a full part of this society and that they've got pathways and avenues to succeed—I think that would be a pretty good outcome from what was obviously a tragic situation. And we're going to spend some time working on that and thinking about that.

And then, finally, I think it's going to be important for all of us to do some soul-searching. There has been talk about should we convene a conversation on race. I haven't seen that be particularly productive when politicians try to organize conversations. They end up being stilted and politicized, and folks are locked into the positions they already have. On the other hand, in families and churches and workplaces, there's the possibility that people are a little bit more honest, and at least you ask yourself your own questions about, am I wringing as much bias out of myself as I can? Am I judging people as much as I can, based on not the color of their skin, but the content of their character? That would, I think, be an appropriate exercise in the wake of this tragedy.

And let me just leave you with a final thought that, as difficult and challenging as this whole episode has been for a lot of people, I don't want us to lose sight that things are getting better. Each successive generation seems to be making progress in changing attitudes when it comes to race. It doesn't mean we're in a post-racial society. It doesn't mean that racism is eliminated. But when I talk to Malia and Sasha, and I listen to their friends and I see them interact, they're better than we are—they're better than we were—on these issues. And that's true in every community that I've visited all across the country.

And so we have to be vigilant and we have to work on these issues. And those of us in authority should be doing everything we can to encourage the better angels of our nature, as opposed to using these episodes to heighten divisions. But we should also have confidence that kids these days, I think, have more sense than we did back then, and certainly more than our parents did or our grandparents did; and that along this long, difficult journey, we're becoming a more perfect union—not a perfect union, but a more perfect union.

Facing Facts About Race

Victor Davis Hanson

Victor Davis Hanson is the Martin and Illie Anderson Senior Fellow at the Hoover Institution.

Last week President Obama weighed in again on the Trayvon Martin episode. Sadly, most of what he said was wrong, both literally and ethically.

Pace the president, the Zimmerman case was not about Stand Your Ground laws. It was not a white-on-black episode. The shooting involved a Latino of mixed heritage in a violent altercation with a black youth.

Is it ethical for the president to weigh in on a civil-rights case apparently being examined by his own Justice Department? The president knows that if it is true that African-American males are viewed suspiciously, it is probably because statistically they commit a disproportionate amount of violent crime. If that were not true, they might well be given no more attention as supposed suspects than is accorded to white, Asian, or Latino youths. Had George Zimmerman been black, he would have been, statistically at least, *more* likely to have shot Trayvon Martin—and statistically likewise less likely to have been tried.

Barack Obama knows that if non-African-Americans were to cease all inordinate scrutiny of young African-American males, the latter's inordinate crime rates would probably not be affected—given other causation for disproportionate incidences of criminality. Yet should their statistical crime profiles suddenly resemble those of other racial and ethnic groups, the so-called profiling would likely cease.

The president, I think, spoke out for three reasons: 1) He is an unbound, lame-duck president, with a ruined agenda, facing mounting ethical scandals; from now on, he will say things more consonant with being a community organizer than with being a nation's president; 2) he knows the federal civil-rights case has little merit and cannot be pursued, and thus wanted to shore up his bona fides with an aggrieved black community; and 3) as with the ginned-up "assault-weapons ban" and the claim that Republicans are waging a "war on women," Obama knows, as a community activist, that tension can mask culpability—in his case, the utter failure to address soaring unemployment in the inner city, epidemic black murder rates, the bankruptcy of Detroit, and the ways his failed economic policies disproportionately affect inner-city youth.

Attorney General Eric Holder earlier gave an address to the NAACP on the Zimmerman trial. His oration was likewise not aimed at binding wounds. Apparently he wanted to re-mind his anguished audience that because of the acquittal of Zimmerman, there still is not racial justice in America.

Holder noted in lamentation that he had to repeat to his own son the lecture that his father long ago gave him. The sermon was about the dangers of police stereotyping of young black males. Apparently, Holder believes that the more things change, the more they stay the same.

Yet I fear that for every lecture of the sort that Holder is forced to give his son, millions of non-African-Americans are offering their own versions of ensuring safety to their progeny.

In my case, the sermon—aside from constant reminders to judge a man on his merits, not on his class or race—was very precise.

First, let me say that my father was a lifelong Democrat. He had helped to establish a local junior college aimed at pro-viding vocational education for at-risk minorities, and as a hands-on administrator he found himself on some occasions in a physical altercation with a disaffected student. In middle age, he and my mother once were parking their car on a visit to San Francisco when they were suddenly surrounded by several African-American teens. When confronted with their demands, he offered to give the thieves all his cash if they would leave him and my mother alone. Thankfully they took his cash and left.

There are two narratives about race in America, and increasingly they have nothing to do with each other.

I think that experience—and others—is why he once advised me, "When you go to San Francisco, be careful if a group of black youths approaches you." Note what he did *not* say to me. He did not employ language like "typical black person." He did not advise extra caution about black women, the elderly, or the very young—or about young Asian Punjabi, or Native American males. In other words, the advice was not about race per se, but instead about the tendency of males of one particular age and race to commit an inordinate amount of violent crime.

It was after some first-hand episodes with young African-American males that I offered a similar lecture to my own son. The advice was born out of experience rather than subjective stereotyping. When I was a graduate student living in East Palo Alto, two adult black males once tried to break through the door of my apartment—while I was in it. On a second occasion, four black males attempted to steal my bicycle—while I was on it. I could cite three more examples that more or less conform to the same apprehensions once expressed by a younger Jesse Jackson. Regrettably, I expect that my son already has his own warnings prepared to pass on to his own future children.

Holder, of course, knows that there are two narratives about race in America, and increasingly they have nothing to do with each other. In one, African-Americans understandably cite racism and its baleful legacy to explain vast present-day disparities in income, education, and rates of criminality. Others often counter by instead emphasizing the wages of an inner-city culture of single-parent families and government dependence, and the glorification of violence in the popular media.

In the old days of the Great Society, we once dreamed of splitting the difference—the government would invest more in the inner city, while black leadership in turn would emphasize more self-help and self-critique.

Not now. Both sides have almost given up on persuading the other. Eric Holder's speech to the NAACP might as well have been given on Mars. It will convince zero Americans that stereotyping of young African-American males and Stand Your Ground laws are the two key racial problems facing America.

Again, Holder may offer his 15-year-old son the same warning that his father gave him about the dangers of racist, stereotyping police. Yet I suspect—and statistics would again support such supposition—that Holder privately is more worried that his son is in greater danger of being attacked by other black youths than by either the police or a nation of white-Hispanic George Zimmermans on the loose.

There is no evidence in our increasingly self-segregated society that white liberals stand out as integrationists.

Besides, two developments over recent decades have made Holder's reactionary argument about black/white relations mostly irrelevant. First, America is now a multiracial nation. The divide is not white versus black. And as the Zimmerman trial reminds us, it is no longer a nation where most of the authority figures are white males. We saw a female judge, a female jury, and an Hispanic in confrontation with an African-

American; today those of various racial pedigrees and different genders interact in ways that transcend the supposed culpability of white males.

Second, the attitude of the so-called white community toward racial challenges is not so much political as class driven. White liberals have largely won the argument that massive government expenditure must be infused into the black community. Yet they have probably lost the argument that such vast government investments have done much to alleviate the plight of urban black youth.

Stranger still, there is no evidence in our increasingly self-segregated society that white liberals stand out as integrationists. The latter increasingly have the capital to school their children far from the inner city, to live largely apart from inner-city blacks, and in general to avoid the black underclass in the concrete as much as they profess liberal nostrums for it in the abstract.

No one seems to care that the children of our liberal elite, black and white, go to places like Sidwell Friends rather than to Washington public schools, where the consequences of 50 years of liberal social policy are all too real. If Chris Matthews wishes to apologize collectively for whites, then he should have long ago moved to an integrated neighborhood, put his children in integrated schools, and walked to work through a black neighborhood to get to know local residents. Anything else, and his apology remains what it is: cheap psychological recompense for his own elite apartheid.

Just as Eric Holder preferred anecdote to statistics, so too I end with an unscientific vignette of my own. Last week I was driving in northern California with the attorney general's speech playing on the car radio. North of San Francisco I stopped to buy coffee and two local newspapers.

In one, there was a gruesome story of a young African-American male charged with ransacking a San Francisco jewelry store and murdering two employees, Khin Min, 35, of San

Francisco, and Lina Lim, 51, of Daly City. The owner of the shop, Vic Hung, fought back and survived, despite receiving gunshot and stab wounds in the attack.

The suspected attacker had a prior record of violent assault. The victims were all of Asian ancestry. I don't think their families would agree with Eric Holder that self-defense laws were the cause of such interracial violence. Nor would the six policemen who were fired upon by the suspect agree that stereotyping prompted this sort of mayhem.

Barack Obama will never suggest that the suspected killer physically resembles himself some three decades ago—and there would be no point in doing so. Nor will he admit that if Barack Obama owned an urban jewelry store and needed its profits to send his daughters to Sidwell Friends, he too might have become apprehensive when a young black male entered his store.

In the other paper, there was a strangely similar tale. Not far away, in Santa Rosa, at about the same time, two African-American youths in hoodies attacked another jewelry store, also had a shoot-out with the owner, and also failed to evade the police—though in this case none of the employees or customers was injured.

In such cases, too many Americans find there is a sort of tired sameness. The victims were white or Asian. The murder and robbery suspects were young African-American males. The violence was aimed not at acquiring food or clothing, but at stealing luxury goods. The armed small-business owners tried to defend themselves by firing back at their attackers. Had they been unarmed, both would have probably perished. In one case, the police were fired upon. The suspects had prior arrests.

And on and on and on across America each day, this same tragedy is played out of a small percentage of Americans committing violent crimes at rates far exceeding their proportion of the general population.

The world will long remember Trayvon Martin, but few people—and certainly not Barack Obama or Eric Holder, who have a bad habit, in an increasingly multiracial country, of claiming solidarity on the basis of race—will care that Khin Min and Lina Lim were torn to pieces by bullets and a knife. Few will care that they died in a vicious assault that had nothing to do with stereotyping, Stand Your Ground self-defense, weak gun laws, insufficient federal civil-rights legislation, or any of the other causes of interracial violence falsely advanced by the attorney general—but quite a lot to do with an urban culture that for unspoken reasons has spawned an epidemic of disproportionate violent crime on the part of young African-American males.

I offer one final surreal footnote to this strange juxtaposition of reading the real news while listening to the mythohistory that a Eric Holder constructed from the death of Trayvon Martin to indict both the police and the public.

What were the names of two of the men suspected of being the ones who last week shot it out with the Santa Rosa jeweler as Eric Holder demagogued the Trayvon Martin shooting?

Traveon Banks-Austin and Alexander Tyvon Brandon.

And so the tragedy continues.

There Is a Need for the End Racial Profiling Act

Benjamin L. Cardin

Benjamin L. Cardin is a Democratic US senator representing the state of Maryland.

Over the past few months the nation's attention has been riveted to the tragic, avoidable death of Trayvon Martin in Florida. A few weeks ago I spoke about this issue at the Center for Urban Families in Baltimore.

Joining me were representatives from various faith and civil rights groups in Baltimore, as well as graduates from the Center's program. I heard there first-hand accounts of typical American families that were victims of racial profiling. One young woman recounted going to a basketball game with her father, only to have her dad detained by police for no apparent reason other than the color of his skin.

Questions About Martin's Death

That's why I am pleased that the Justice Department, under the supervision of Attorney General Eric Holder, has announced an investigation into the shooting death of Trayvon Martin on February 26, 2012. As we all know from the news, an unarmed Martin, 17, was shot in Sanford, FL on his way home from a convenience store by Mr. George Zimmerman.

I join all Americans in wanting a full and complete investigation into the shooting death of Trayvon Martin to ensure that justice is served. There are many questions that we need the Justice Department to answer.

Benjamin L. Cardin, Testimony of Benjamin L. Cardin, US Senator, Hearing on "Ending Racial Profiling in America," Senate Judiciary Committee, Subcommittee on the Constitution, Civil Rights, and Human Rights, US Senate, April 17, 2012.

Was Trayvon targeted by Mr. Zimmerman because he was black? The state of Florida has already charged Zimmerman with second-degree murder, and Zimmerman will be given a jury trial of his peers to determine whether he is guilty [he was acquitted in July 2013].

A key question is whether Trayvon was a victim of racial profiling by the police. Was Trayvon treated differently by local law enforcement in their shooting investigation because he was black and the aggressor was white?

Trayvon's tragic death leads to a discussion of the broader issue of racial profiling. I have called for putting an end to racial profiling, a practice that singles out individuals based on race or other protected categories. In October 2011, I introduced legislation, *End Racial Profiling Act* (ERPA), S. 1670, which would protect minority communities by prohibiting the use of racial profiling by law enforcement officials.

The End Racial Profiling Act

First, the bill prohibits the use of racial profiling—using a standard definition—that includes race, ethnicity, national origin, or religion. All law enforcement agencies would be prohibited from using racial profiling in criminal or routine law enforcement investigations, immigration enforcement, and national security cases.

The bill also prohibits the use of race in "deciding upon the scope and substance of law enforcement activity following the initial investigatory procedure."

Second, the bill would mandate training on racial profiling issues, and requires data collection by local and state law enforcement agencies.

Third, this bill would condition the receipt of federal funds by state and local law enforcement on two grounds. First, under this bill, state and local law enforcement would have to "maintain adequate policies and procedures designed to eliminate racial profiling." Second, they must "eliminate any existing practices that permit or encourage racial profiling."

Fourth, the bill would authorize the Justice Department to provide grants to state and local government to develop and implement best policing practices that would discourage racial profiling.

Finally, the bill would require the Attorney General to provide periodic reports to assess the nature of any ongoing discriminatory profiling practices.

The bill would also provide remedies for individuals who were harmed by racial profiling.

Racial profiling is bad policy, but given the state of our budgets, it also diverts scarce resources from real law enforcement.

Support for New Legislation

The legislation I introduced is supported by the NAACP [National Association for the Advancement of Colored People], ACLU [American Civil Liberties Union], the Rights Working Group, and the Leadership Conference on Civil and Human Rights, and numerous other organizations.

I thank these groups and many others for their efforts in putting a human face on the issue of racial profiling, and for the numerous reports they have issued on the different faces of racial profiling, which I encourage Senators to review. I strongly support their advocacy efforts on Capitol Hill this week to raise awareness of this issue and build co-sponsors for this legislation. I ask unanimous consent to include a letter in the record from numerous civil rights and human rights organizations endorsing this legislation.

Let me also thank Chairman [Dick] Durbin for leading the effort in the Senate on a letter to Attorney General Holder asking him to revise the Department of Justice's racial profiling guidance.

Racial profiling is bad policy, but given the state of our budgets, it also diverts scarce resources from real law enforcement. Law enforcement officials nationwide already have tight budgets. The more resources spent investigating individuals solely because of their race or religion, the fewer resources directed at suspects who are actually demonstrating illegal behavior.

Racial profiling has no place in modern law enforcement. The vast majority of our law enforcement officials who put their lives on the line every day handle their jobs with professionalism, diligence, and fidelity to the rule of law. However, Congress and the Justice Department can and should still take steps to prohibit racial profiling and finally root out its use.

The Fourteenth Amendment to the U.S. Constitution guarantees the "equal protection of the laws" to all Americans. Racial profiling is abhorrent to that principle, and should be ended once and for all.

As the late Senator [Ted] Kennedy often said, "Civil Rights is the great unfinished business of America." Let's continue the fight here to make sure that we truly have equal justice under law for all Americans.

There Is No Need for the End Racial Profiling Act

Roger Clegg

Roger Clegg is the president and general counsel of the Center for Equal Opportunity, a conservative think tank devoted to issues of race and ethnicity.

M y name is Roger Clegg, and I am president and general counsel of the Center for Equal Opportunity, a nonprofit research and educational organization that is based in Falls Church, Virginia. Our chairman is Linda Chavez, and our focus is on public policy issues that involve race and ethnicity, such as civil rights, bilingual education, and immigration and assimilation. I should also note that I was a deputy in the U.S. Department of Justice's Civil Rights Division for four years, from 1987 to 1991.

In my testimony today, I want to make these points: (1) care must be taken in defining the term "racial profiling"; (2) the amount of racial profiling that occurs is frequently exaggerated, and care must be taken in analyzing the data in this area; (3) with those caveats, racial profiling as I will define it is a bad policy and I oppose it, with (4) a possible exception in some antiterrorism contexts; but (5) there are problems with trying to legislate in this area in general, and the End Racial Profiling Act in particular is problematic.

The Definition of Racial Profiling

Racial profiling occurs when race is used as a criterion in deciding whom to investigate, unless there is evidence that a particular crime was committed by someone of a particular race.

Roger Clegg, Testimony of Roger Clegg, President and General Counsel, Center for Equal Opportunity, Hearing on "Ending Racial Profiling in America," Senate Judiciary Committee, Subcommittee on the Constitution, Civil Rights, and Human Rights, US Senate, April 17, 2012.

So, for example, it is not racial profiling if the police focus their efforts in high-crime areas, even if the residents of those areas are disproportionately one color or another. It is not racial profiling if the police respond to citizen complaints, say, about drug sales in a neighborhood, even if those neighborhoods turn out, again, to be disproportionately one color or another.

Also, it is not racial profiling if the victim of a mugging has described the assailant as someone who is six-feet tall, weighs 200 pounds, has a beard, was wearing a red windbreaker, and is a middle-aged white male—and so the police consider all those characteristics, including race, in questioning people.

Rather, a classic instance of racial profiling would occur if the police decided to pull over cars just exceeding the speed limit on I-95 if but only if they were late-model cars driven by a male driver with one or two passengers, and only if the driver was black, because the police thought that such cars were more likely to be involved in drug trafficking.

If some groups in the aggregate commit crimes at statistically higher rates than other groups, then we would of course expect racial disproportions in investigations, arrests, and convictions.

Note, by the way, that the fact that characteristics besides race are considered—whether the car was speeding, was relatively new, and had one or two passengers—does not mean that racial profiling has not occurred. So long as race is *a* factor, it is not necessary that it be the *only* factor.

In this regard, let me note that the Center for Equal Opportunity's position is consistent when race is considered in university admissions. The fact that race is not the *only* factor considered does not mean that discrimination has not occurred, so long as it is *a* factor. I won't belabor the point today, but it is remarkable that frequently the same organizations and the same people who are outraged about racial profiling when it is done by the police are perfectly happy with it when it is done by university admission officials.

The Frequency of Racial Profiling

Care must be taken in analyzing data in order to determine if racial profiling has occurred. There can obviously be a problem here if racial profiling is not defined rigorously in the first place, as I have already discussed. But there can be problems even if it is.

For example, suppose that 80 percent of the cars driven along a particular route that are *stopped* by the police are driven by men, but that only 50 percent of all the cars *driven* along the route are driven by men. Is this evidence that men are being singled out by the police for stops? Not if men are much more likely to exceed the speed limit than women are. By the same token, if some members of some groups are more likely than members of some other groups to attract the attention of the police for nonracial reasons (like speeding), the fact that there are racial disproportions in police stops may not be persuasive evidence—let alone proof—that discrimination has occurred. And, of course, if some groups in the aggregate commit crimes at statistically higher rates than other groups, then we would of course expect racial disproportions in investigations, arrests, and convictions, too. Again, if most street crime is committed by men, then of course a disproportionate number of investigations, arrests, and convictions will involve men. And it cannot be seriously argued that all racial and ethnic groups at all times will commit all types of crimes at the same rates.

I am not going to argue that racial profiling never occurs. With all the law-enforcement officials in this country, it would be astonishing if some of them—and of all colors, by the way—did not sometimes consider race or ethnicity consciously or unconsciously in deciding whom to investigate.

But I will say that the amount of racial profiling that takes place has frequently been exaggerated. In this regard, I would refer the committee in particular to the work of Heather Mac Donald of the Manhattan Institute in this area.

Racial Profiling Is Bad Policy

To the extent that racial profiling *does* occur in traditional law-enforcement contexts, however, it is a bad policy and I oppose it.

Some would argue that racial profiling is perfectly rational and ought therefore to be unobjectionable. The argument is that a disproportionate amount of street crime is committed by people who are young, and male, and black, and if you are all three then it makes perfect sense for the police to keep an especially keen eye on you, and pull you over more often, question you more carefully, and press you more aggressively to allow a search of your car. That is, it makes perfect sense if all the police are trying to do is maximize in the short term the number of their successful searches and arrests.

I think that racial profiling is inconsistent with the principle of E pluribus unum—*that we are all Americans and none of us ought to be treated differently on the basis of skin color or national origin.*

But that is not the police's overarching mission. They have to think of the long-term, too, and successful policing requires the cooperation of the rest of the community. If racially biased policing is an established policy, then that cooperation will be jeopardized.

Moreover, the order which the police are charged with maintaining includes not just the prevention of crime but the racially unbiased treatment of law-abiding citizens. It is simply un-American for the government to be treating some Americans differently from other Americans because of skin color or what country their ancestors came from.

I've already drawn an analogy between racial profiling by the police and racial profiling by university admission officials. Here's another analogy: Suppose that a city agency is interested in hiring only people with a high-school diploma, and in that city the overwhelming majority of whites have a diploma and the overwhelming majority of Hispanics don't. Rather than have to go to the trouble of checking out the records of each applicant, it may be much more cost-efficient simply to hire all whites and no Hispanics. But most of us would insist that each applicant be assessed individually. (Clearly, that is what the law requires.) Cost-efficient hiring is important to the city, but not so important as to justify racial discrimination.

In sum, I think that racial profiling is inconsistent with the principle of *E pluribus unum* [out of many, one]—that we are all Americans and none of us ought to be treated differently on the basis of skin color or national origin.

The Possible Exception in the Terrorism Context

On the other hand, if in a particular case racial profiling might save the lives of thousands of people, it should be permitted. If, for example, considering someone's national origin would make it more likely that law-enforcement officials could thwart a terrorist plot to detonate a bomb in a U.S. city, I would not oppose it.

But, having said that, let me note that I am not sure if this is generally the case in the war on terror, and I am also not sure that it would necessarily be racial profiling.

Let me explain the second point first. Earlier I made the point that, if you are mugged by a six-foot, 200-pound, middle-aged white male wearing a red windbreaker, it is not "racial profiling" for the police to be on the lookout for people who meet that description, even though one element in it is racial. The classic case of racial profiling is, instead, when the police decide to stop cars being driven by young black males, not because they have the description of a specific suspect, but because they know that statistically drugs are more likely to be smuggled by young black males than, say, old Asian females.

But there are other circumstances that fall in between these two extremes. Suppose, for instance, that you are looking for members of a particular, Berlin-based drug cartel, who are engaged in particular acts of smuggling, and you know that they will all be German nationals, but you don't have specific names or descriptions that go beyond that. Is it "racial profiling" for the police to give shorter shrift in their investigation to people who are less likely to be Germans—to, say, Asians and African Americans?

It is hard for me to believe that, if we are fighting an enemy with a particular religious/geopolitical agenda, that it won't make sense to be on the lookout for people who share those religious/geopolitical ties.

Enough hypotheticals. Suppose that you have already identified several members of a terrorist ring and want to find the rest. The ones you have identified so far meet a particular profile: Middle Eastern ties. Muslim. Several are trained pilots. Male. Young or middle-aged. Booked on transcontinental flights. What's more, the ring is avowedly Islamist and anti-Israeli. Any problem with assuming that there is a good chance that the remaining members of the ring are likely to meet this profile, too?

This is a lot closer to the "specific description" extreme of the spectrum than the "statistically speaking" end of the spectrum. Which means that this really isn't properly characterized as racial profiling at all. This doesn't mean you ignore every-one who doesn't meet the profile or shoot to kill anyone with black hair. But you look harder at those who fit the descrip-tion.

And the other response is, so what if it *is* racial profiling? No one believes that the government should never, under any circumstances, consider race in its actions.

Allowable Racial Classifications

Suppose, for example, that on 9/11 [2001] the FBI [Federal Bureau of Investigation] had received information that a ter-rorist on a jetliner that had been grounded had, as an alterna-tive plan, loaded a private plane with explosives that he now intended to crash into a skyscraper. As the FBI frantically looked over the passenger lists of the grounded planes—with limited time and resources—would anyone argue that it ought to be forbidden from focusing first on those individuals with Arabic names? More broadly, it is hard for me to believe that, if we are fighting an enemy with a particular religious/ geopolitical agenda, that it won't make sense to be on the lookout for people who share those religious/geopolitical ties.

As the Supreme Court has said, the Constitution is not a suicide pact. And thus one would not expect it to bar the gov-ernment from doing what is necessary to defend the ordered liberty of our society. Racial classifications are allowed if they are "narrowly tailored" to a "compelling governmental inter-est," according to the Supreme Court's case law. If stopping terrorism is not a compelling interest, then nothing is.

Note that the distinctions I am drawing here are reflected in the U.S. Justice Department's "Guidance Regarding the Use of Race by Federal Law Enforcement Agencies."

Let me stress, however, that even if ethnicity is used in this context, it ought to be used as sparingly as possible, for two reasons. First, it can be lazy and inefficient to use ethnicity as a proxy for behavior, as Professor Nelson Lund has argued in opposing my defense of the Justice Department's guidance. This problem is exacerbated by the fact that terrorists can always recruit members of nonprofiled groups. And, second, the high costs of profiling that I discussed before—the abridgment of the principle of *E pluribus unum* and the risk of alienating the law-abiding people whose cooperation is essential in the war on terror—remain. If racial profiling can be avoided, if there are better ways to identify potential terrorists, then that is the better course.

If it's an easy and more fool-proof procedure to send everyone through the metal detector rather than to pick and choose whom to send through, then send everyone through. That's a small price to pay to avoid government use of racial classifications. Conversely, if closer searches are required for some and ethnicity is one element in that decision, then *that* is a small price to be paid to minimize the risk of getting blown up, and the people being searched should show some patience. It's *their* safety that is being ensured, too, after all.

Problems with Legislating in This Area

While I am no fan of racial profiling, I am skeptical about whether it makes sense for a legislature to try to codify appropriate behavior in this area. As I hope my testimony so far has shown, there are a lot of nuances here that are difficult to write into a one-size-fits-all law that is supposed to apply permanently to all law-enforcement agencies at every level of all governments. For example, it would be hard to articulate where the line is to be drawn between ordinary criminal activity and the extraordinary threats posed by extremist groups, and there is also a gray area in situations where not every individual in a criminal enterprise has been racially identified but the enterprise itself nonetheless has a racial (or ethnic or religious) identity of sorts. I'm also skeptical about the courts playing an efficacious role in this area (the End Racial Profiling Act is designed to encourage litigation, by providing for attorney and expert fees and making it easy to make out a *prima facie* [on its face, accepted as correct until proven otherwise] case).

It is critically important that legitimate, nondiscriminatory police strategies that nonetheless have a disproportionate impact on one group or another not be discouraged.

This is not to say that this is a matter where there is no role for anyone except the police themselves. I think that oversight hearings—with accompanying political and community pressure—can make sense if done responsibly, as well as of course self-policing and, in extreme cases, investigations by the U.S. Department of Justice's civil rights division.

I hasten to add that all of this ought to be done with a lot of sympathy and support for the tough and dangerous job that the police have to do, and with recognition of the fact that racial disparities do not equal racial discrimination. If the police are hamstrung, those who will be hurt the most will be law-abiding people in high-crime areas—people who are themselves likely to be poor and African American.

And, finally, while I am no fan of racial profiling, I am also no fan of the "disparate impact" approach to civil-rights enforcement and therefore no fan of this part of the End Racial Profiling Act in particular.

It is critically important that legitimate, nondiscriminatory police strategies that nonetheless have a disproportionate impact on one group or another not be discouraged. Alas, this bill does that in two ways. First, it mandates data collection by beat cops, which would inevitably pressure them to stop (or not stop) people in such a way that they "get their numbers right." Second, it explicitly declares that "a disparate impact on racial, ethnic, or religious minorities shall constitute *prima facie* evidence of a violation of this title." Note also that this provision, ironically, makes the bill itself of dubious constitutionality, since it explicitly accepts law-enforcement activities that have a disparate impact on some racial, ethnic, and religious groups, but not those that have a disparate impact on others. The End Racial Profiling Act, in other words, literally denies the equal protection of the laws and uses racial profiling.

Proposed Prohibitions on Racial Profiling Will Hinder Law Enforcement

Linda Chavez

Linda Chavez is chairman of the Center for Equal Opportunity, a conservative think tank devoted to issues of race and ethnicity.

Racial profiling, which has always been a thorny issue, is about to get a lot more complicated. In a private meeting with New York City Mayor Bill de Blasio, Attorney General Eric Holder this week [January 15, 2014] promised that the Department of Justice soon will issue long-anticipated new rules expanding the definition of what constitutes racial profiling.

De Blasio made his opposition to the city's tough "stop and frisk" policies a central theme in his successful campaign, alleging that the practice constitutes harassment of racial minorities. And Holder apparently agrees. Now, Holder plans to prohibit federal investigators from considering not only race, but also sex, religion, national origin and sexual orientation. What's more, Holder is expected to broaden federal prohibitions on profiling beyond criminal justice to include counterterrorism investigations, surveillance and immigration enforcement.

The Definition of Racial Profiling

I have always opposed racial profiling. In my view, government shouldn't be choosing winners or losers on the basis of skin color. I think it's wrong to use race to determine whom to hire or admit to college—and also wrong to single out minorities for sobriety, drug or weapons checks. It seems quite consistent to oppose both racial preferences that advantage minorities and racial profiling that disadvantages them. But it is important to be clear on what we mean by racial profiling and how we go about proving it.

There are several problems with the new rules. First, the Holder Justice Department in general views discrimination so broadly that policies that have an adverse impact on minorities are often deemed discriminatory even if there is no intent to discriminate and the policies themselves are neutral. By definition, racial profiling would seem to imply intent. But given its history, the Holder Justice Department [DOJ] might decide that any policing policy that results in a disproportionate impact on minorities will be seen as profiling.

An important study of racial profiling completed in 2002, for example, noted that minority neighborhoods often have a higher police presence because they also experience higher crime rates, which will lead to more stops of minority individuals. "Studies that do not consider these and other police operational procedures, along with additional specific city characteristics, will fail to accurately assess the existence or extent of racial profiling or bias-based policing," the study said. Yet one can imagine the Holder DOJ using exactly such flawed statistics to show widespread racial profiling.

In addition, expanding the prohibited categories to include not only race and color, but also national origin, religion and even sex will complicate both counterterrorism and immigration enforcement.

The Importance of Exceptions

President George W. Bush banned racial profiling in federal law enforcement in 2003, but he applied the ban only to racial and ethnic profiling and carved out exemptions for terrorism and national security. The new regulations are expected to reverse those exemptions, which will make the fight against terrorism more difficult.

One of the reasons that the Bush administration allowed investigators to profile based on national origin and religion was that both factors were relevant in counterterrorism. The administration made the exceptions less than two years after 19 terrorists attacked the United States, all of them foreign-born Islamists. It would have been irresponsible for the Bush administration not to take religion and national origin into account in looking for those likely to commit new acts of terrorism.

In fact, the chief criticism of security measures at airports and other places in the wake of 9/11 [2001] is that there hasn't been enough profiling. Does it really make sense to subject a 75-year-old woman from Kansas to the same level of scrutiny as a 25-year-old male from Yemen? It makes sense to pay closer attention to some people than others if you have limited resources. Some would call that discernment, not discrimination.

Holder's proposals have garnered praise from those in the civil rights and civil liberties community and in some Arab and Muslim organizations. But they are likely to weaken national security, make policing more difficult and making all Americans—including minorities—less safe in their own communities.

Organizations to Contact

The editors have compiled the following list of organizations concerned with the issues debated in this book. The descriptions are derived from materials provided by the organizations. All have publications or information available for interested readers. The list was compiled on the date of publication of the present volume; the information provided here may change. Be aware that many organizations take several weeks or longer to respond to inquiries, so allow as much time as possible.

American Civil Liberties Union (ACLU)
125 Broad St., 18th Floor, New York, NY   10004
(212) 549-2500
website: www.aclu.org

The American Civil Liberties Union is a national organization that works to defend Americans' civil rights as guaranteed in the US Constitution. The ACLU Immigrants' Rights Project is dedicated to expanding and enforcing the civil liberties and civil rights of noncitizens, and to combating public and private discrimination against immigrants. The ACLU publishes the semiannual newsletter *Civil Liberties Alert* as well as briefing papers, including the publication "Immigration Myths and Facts."

Amnesty International USA
5 Penn Plaza, New York, NY   10001
(212) 807-8400 • fax: (212) 627-1451
website: www.amnestyusa.org

Founded in 1961, Amnesty International is a grassroots activist organization that aims to free all nonviolent people who have been imprisoned because of their beliefs, ethnic origin, race, or gender. Amnesty International USA makes its reports, press releases, and fact sheets available through its website, including the report "Threat and Humiliation: Racial Profiling, National Security, and Human Rights in the United States."

Cato Institute

1000 Massachusetts Ave. NW, Washington, DC   20001-5403
(202) 842-0200 • fax: (202) 842-3490
website: www.cato.org

The Cato Institute is a public policy research foundation dedicated to limiting the role of government, protecting individual liberties, and promoting free markets. The institute commissions a variety of publications, including books, monographs, briefing papers, and other studies. Among its publications are the quarterly magazine *Regulation*, the bimonthly *Cato Policy Report*, and articles such as "When Will America End Racial Bias?"

Council on American-Islamic Relations (CAIR)

453 New Jersey Ave. SE, Washington, DC   20003
(202) 488-8787 • fax: (202) 488-0833
website: www.cair.com

The Council on American-Islamic Relations is a Muslim civil liberties and advocacy group focused on both bridging the gap between Muslim and non-Muslim Americans and protecting the rights of Muslims in the United States. CAIR regularly meets and works with law enforcement and members of the federal, state, and local governments in order to facilitate communication with US Muslim communities to raise awareness of issues affecting Muslims. The CAIR website includes reports, surveys, public service announcements, and press releases on issues of specific concern to American Muslims and on Islam-related topics of general interest.

National Association for the Advancement of Colored People (NAACP)

4805 Mt. Hope Dr., Baltimore, MD   21215
(877) 622-2798
website: www.naacp.org

Founded one hundred years ago, the National Association for the Advancement of Colored People is the oldest civil rights organization in the United States. Its primary focus is the protection and enhancement of the civil rights of African Americans and other minorities. Working at the national, regional, and local levels, the organization educates the public on the adverse effects of discrimination, advocates legislation, and monitors enforcement of existing civil rights laws. NAACP publishes *Crisis*, a bimonthly magazine, and provides press releases on its website.

National Urban League (NUL)
120 Wall St., New York, NY   10005
(212) 558-5300 • fax: (212) 344-5332
website: www.nul.iamempowered.com

A community service agency, the National Urban League's mission is to eliminate institutional racism in the United States. It also provides services for minorities who experience discrimination in employment, housing, welfare, and other areas. It publishes the report "The Price: A Study of the Costs of Racism in America," the annual "State of Black America," and other documents that deal with the issues of racism and discrimination.

US Department of Homeland Security (DHS)
245 Murray Lane SW, Washington, DC   20528
(202) 282-8000
website: www.dhs.gov

Created in 2002 following the September 11, 2001, terrorist attacks on the United States, the US Department of Homeland Security serves as a coordinating agency providing information about potential threats to America and its citizens, as well as offers tactical options to take action and prevent further harmful events. Publications such as "Commitment to Race Neutrality in Law Enforcement Activities" are available on its website.

US Department of Justice (DOJ)
950 Pennsylvania Ave. NW, Washington, DC   20530-0001
(202) 514-2000

e-mail: AskDOJ@usdoj.gov
website: www.usdoj.gov

The mission of the US Department of Justice is to enforce the law and defend the interests of the United States according to the law; to ensure public safety against foreign and domestic threats; to provide federal leadership in preventing and controlling crime; to seek just punishment for those guilty of unlawful behavior; and to ensure fair and impartial administration of justice for all Americans. Publications available on its website include "Guidance Regarding the Use of Race by Federal Law Enforcement Agencies" as well as articles about current DOJ activities and links to DOJ agencies such as the Civil Rights Division.

Bibliography

Books

Martha R. Bireda	*Cultures in Conflict: Eliminating Racial Profiling.* Lanham, MD: Rowman & Littlefield, 2010.
Michael L. Birzer	*Racial Profiling: They Stopped Me Because I'm—.* Boca Raton, FL: CRC Press, 2013.
David Boonin	*Should Race Matter? Unusual Answers to the Usual Questions.* New York: Cambridge University Press, 2011.
Joseph Collum	*The Black Dragon: Racial Profiling Exposed.* Sun River, MT: Jigsaw Press, 2010.
Elizabeth Comack	*Racialized Policing: Aboriginal People's Encounters with the Police.* Winnipeg, Canada: Fernwood Publishing, 2012.
Anthony Cortese	*Contentious: Immigration, Affirmative Action, Racial Profiling, and the Death Penalty.* Austin, TX: University of Texas Press, 2013.
Alejandro del Carmen	*Racial Profiling in America.* Upper Saddle River, NJ: Pearson Prentice Hall, 2008.
Karen S. Glover	*Racial Profiling: Research, Racism, and Resistance.* Lanham, MD: Rowman & Littlefield, 2009.

Amaney Jamal and Nadine Naber, eds.	*Race and Arab Americans Before and After 9/11: From Invisible Citizens to Visible Subjects.* Syracuse, NY: Syracuse University Press, 2008.
Cynthia Lee	*The Fourth Amendment: Searches and Seizures, Its Constitutional History and the Contemporary Debate.* Amherst, NY: Prometheus Books, 2010.
Gregory S. Parks and Matthew W. Hughey, eds.	*12 Angry Men: True Stories of Being a Black Man in America Today.* New York: New Press, 2010.
Stephen K. Rice and Michael D. White, eds.	*Race, Ethnicity, and Policing: New and Essential Readings.* New York: New York University Press, 2010.
Stephen J. Schulhofer	*More Essential than Ever: The Fourth Amendment in the Twenty-First Century.* New York: Oxford University Press, 2012.
Jeff Shantz, ed.	*Racial Profiling and Borders: International, Interdisciplinary Perspectives.* Lake Mary, FL: Vandeplas, 2010.
Michael Tonry	*Punishing Race: A Continuing American Dilemma.* New York: Oxford University Press, 2011.
Tim Wise	*Colorblind: The Rise of Post-Racial Politics and the Retreat from Racial Equity.* San Francisco: City Lights Books, 2010.

Brian L. Withrow   *The Racial Profiling Controversy: What Every Police Leader Should Know.* Flushing, NY: Looseleaf Law, 2011.

Periodicals and Internet Sources

Arian
Campo-Flores   "Arizona's Immigration Law and Racial Profiling," *Newsweek*, April 26, 2010.

Ta-Nehisi Coates   "It's the Racism, Stupid," *Atlantic*, July 23, 2013.

Ben Eidelson   "Liberals Are Making the Wrong Case Against Racial Profiling," *Salon*, May 9, 2010. www.salon.com.

Justin Elliott   "Racial Profiling on an 'Industrial Scale,'" *Salon*, October 22, 2011. www.salon.com.

Renee Feltz   "A Double Standard on Racial Profiling," *American Prospect*, October 5, 2010.

Conor
Freidersdorf   "Conservative Hypocrisy on Racial Profiling and Affirmative Action," *Atlantic*, July 24, 2013.

Alan Gomez   "Racial Profiling Difficult to Prove, Experts Say," *USA Today*, July 11, 2012.

Braden Goyette   "Racial Profiling Is Ineffective and Wrong, So Why Does It Keep Happening?" Generation Progress, October 7, 2010. www.genprogress .org.

Juan Carlos Hidalgo	"Hispanics and Proposition 19," *Cato at Liberty*, October 29, 2010. www.cato.org.
Kenneth Jost	"Profiling Seen in 'Shopping While Black' Incidents," *CQ Researcher*, November 22, 2013.
Sergey Kadinsky, Tom Namako, and Dan Mangan	"Taxi Big: Fair to Profile," *New York Post*, December 7, 2010.
Aaron Kearney	"Why We Need ERPA: Racial Profiling Lingers Amidst Proof of Targeting," CAIR-Chicago, August 6, 2012. www.cairchicago.org.
Heather Mac Donald	"Fighting Crime Where the Criminals Are," *New York Times*, June 25, 2010.
Nancy Murray	"Profiling in the Age of Total Information Awareness," *Race & Class*, October 2010.
Asra Q. Nomani and Hassan Abbas	"Is Racial or Religious Profiling Ever Justified?" *New York Times Upfront*, April 18, 2011.
Dennis Parker	"Scottsboro Boys Exonerated, but Troubling Legacy Remains for Black Men," American Civil Liberties Union, November 21, 2013. www.aclu.org.
Jim Rankin	"When Good People Are Swept Up with the Bad," *Toronto Star*, February 26, 2010.

Ahmed Rehab   "Why Racial Profiling Makes for
                     Dumb Security," *Huffington Post*,
                     January 7, 2010.
                     www.huffingtonpost.com.

Keeanga-Yamahtta   "A Verdict on Racial Profiling? A
Taylor   Judge Has Ruled Stop-and-Frisk
                     Unconstitutional and Racist. But Will
                     It Stop?" *In These Times*, August 16,
                     2013. www.inthesetimes.com.

Dawud Walid   "End Racial Profiling Act: A Smarter
                     Policy," *Huffington Post*, May 3, 2012.
                     www.huffingtonpost.com.

Index